PRACTICAL MORALITY,

OR, A GUIDE TO MEN AND MANNERS:

CONSISTING OF

LORD CHESTERFIELD'S

ADVICE TO HIS SON.

TO WHICH IS ADDED,

A SUPPLEMENT

Containing Extracts from various Books, recommended
by Lord Chesterfield to Mr. Stanhope.

TOGETHER WITH

THE POLITE PHILOSOPHER;

Or, An Essay on the Art which makes a Man happy in
himself, and agreeable to others:

DR. BLAIR'S ADVICE TO YOUTH ;

DR. FORDYCE ON HONOUR AS A PRINCIPLE;

LORD BURGHLEY'S TEN PRECEPTS TO HIS SON;

DR. FRANKLIN'S WAY TO WEALTH;

AND

POPE'S UNIVERSAL PRAYER.

◆

HARTFORD:
PUBLISHED BY WILLIAM ANDRUS.
1841.

ADVERTISEMENT.

THE very flattering reception which the following work experienced from the Public, through
seven successive editions, has encouraged the Editor to enlarge the plan, and thus render the piece
of more extensive utility.

The abilities of Lord Chesterfield, to inculcate
such precepts as should form the mind and fashion
the manners of youth, are too universally admired
to need encomium. In the Advice of that noble
Earl to his Son, there are to be found such judicious
remarks on men, manners, and things, connected
with so intimate a knowledge of the world, that
the sentiments, considered as maxims, form a very
valuable system of education.

But, as the observations of different writers on
the same subject are mutually illustrative of each
other, to render the following work acceptable, a
variety of Notes are subjoined, extracted from a
small treatise on Politeness, entitled 'Galateo.'—
This exquisite piece was written by the Archbishop
of Benevento, in the sixteenth century, about the
commencement of the reign of Queen Elizabeth;
and it shows (as the English Translator observes)
'to what a degree of refinement, both in manners
and literature, the Italians were arrived, when we
were at a period just emerging from ignorance and
barbarity.' Of this treatise thus described it is only

necessary farther to add, that it has been translated into Latin, as well as the modern languages, and so celebrated is the fame of the author, that, at this day, it is proverbial in Italy to pronounce of an ill-bred man, ' *That he has not read* Galateo.'

Without intending the most distant imputation of plagiarism, it may be presumed that Lord Chesterfield had this very book before him when he wrote his Letters to his Son. The reader who takes the trouble of comparing the extracts from Galateo, now subjoined, with the sentiments of the noble Earl, will most probably be of the same opinion.

That nothing might be wanting to render the following work complete, the Precepts of Lord Burghley to his Son are added, as highly estimable on the subjects of manners and education. The most ordinary sentiments of so dignified a character acquire weight; but when a series of well-digested precepts, the result of great knowledge and extensive experience, are delivered for the guidance of a son in the momentous concerns of life and happiness, the preceptor claims our esteem, and his opinions our reverence.

To the preceding editions of this work, the Marchioness de Lambert's Advice to her Son, and the Moral Reflections of the Duc de la Rochefoucault, were annexed, although omitted to be noticed in the Preface. These pieces are continued in the present edition. But the diffusive, and it is hoped pertinent, extracts from Galateo, together with the Precepts of Lord Burghley to his Son, and the celebrated Dr. Franklin's Way to Wealth, the latter of which is now, *for the third time*, introduced as part of this work, afford so copious an improvement as to give novelty and additional value to

this edition. Should the Public be of the same
opinion, the expectation of the Editor will be am-
ply gratified. So much depends on education, that
scarcely too much can be advanced on the subject;
and even, if it should fail of success, an effort to
benefit the rising generation is highly honourable,
and affords that self-approving hour which is the
best reward of every well-meant endeavour.

With regard to the Polite Philosopher, it may
yet be necessary to add that it was printed originally at Edinburgh (1774), and a part of the edition
sent up to London. The novelty of the title, and,
to say truth, of the performance itself, for it is
written in a manner never before made use of in
our language, recommended it to some, and prejudiced it in the opinion of others; but time, which
is the touchstone of such productions, did justice
to the work, and at last procured it an esteem, not
only here, but abroad.

The intent of the author was to make men ashamed of their vices, by showing them how ridiculous
they were made by them, and how impossible it was
for a bad man to be polite. It may be graver books
have been written on this subject, but few more to
the point; its author being equally skilled in books
and in men, in the dead languages and the living;
and his observations will be generally found true,
and his maxims just.

LORD CHESTERFIELD'S
ADVICE TO HIS SON.

ABSENCE OF MIND.

An absent man is generally either a very weak or a very affected man; he is, however, a very disagreeable man in company. He is defective in all the common offices of civility; he does not enter into the general conversation, but breaks into it from time to time with some starts of his own, as if he waked from a dream. He seems wrapped up in thought, and possibly does not think at all: he does not know his most intimate acquaintance by sight, or answers them as if he were at cross purposes. He leaves his hat in one room, his cane in another, and would probably leave his shoes in a third, if his buckles, though awry, did not save them. This is a sure indication, either of a mind so weak that it cannot bear above one object at a time, or so affected, that it would be supposed to be wholly engrossed by some very great and important objects. Sir Isaac Newton, Mr. Locke, and, perhaps, five or six more since the creation, may have had a right to absence, from the intense thought their investigations required; but such liberties cannot be claimed by, nor will be tolerated in, any other persons.

No man is in any degree fit for either business or conversation, who does not command his attention to the present object, be it what it will. When I see a man absent in mind, I choose to be absent in body; for it is almost impossible for me to stay in the room, as I cannot stand inattention and awkwardness.

I would rather be in company with a dead man, than with an absent one; for if the dead man affords me no pleasure, at least he shows me no contempt; whereas the absent man very plainly, though silently, tells me that he does not think me worth his attention. Besides, an absent man can never make any observations upon the characters, customs, and manners of the company. He may be in the best companies all his lifetime (if they would admit him), and never become the wiser:—we may as well converse with a deaf man, as an absent one. It is indeed a practical blunder to address ourselves to a man who, we plainly perceive, neither hears, minds, nor understands us.*

* It is very unpolite to appear melancholy and thoughtful, and, as it were, absent from the company where you are, and wrapt up in your own reflections; and though, perhaps, this may be allowable in those who for many years have been entirely immersed in the study and contemplation of the liberal arts and sciences, yet, in other people, this is by no means to be tolerated. Nay, such persons would act but prudently, if at those seasons when they are disposed to indulge their own private meditations, they would sequester themselves entirely from the company of other people.

To this it may be added (by the way), that a well-bred man ought to check a disposition to gaping frequently, because this yawning propensity seems to arise from a certain weakness and disgust; when the person, who is thus disposed to be gaping continually, wants to be somewhere else rather than where he now is; and therefore

ATTENTION.

A man is fit for neither business nor pleasure,
who either cannot, or does not, command and direct his attention to the present object, and in some
degree banish, for that time, all other objects from
his thoughts. If at a ball, a supper, or a party of
pleasure, a man were to be solving in his own
mind a problem in Euclid, he would be a very bad
companion, and make a poor figure in that company; or if, in studying a problem in his closet, he

---

appears sick of the conversation and amusements of the
present company.

And, certainly, let a man be ever so much inclined to
gaping, yet, if he is intent upon any agreeable amusement, or engaged in any serious meditation, he easily
gets rid of this propensity: but he who is idle and disen-
gaged from all business, this habit is extremely apt to
creep upon him. Hence it comes to pass, that if any one
person happens to gape in company, who have nothing
else to engage their attention, all the rest usually follow
his example; as if he had put them in mind of doing
what, if they had thought of it, they otherwise intended
to have done. Now, as in the Latin and other languages
a yawning fellow is synonymous or equivalent to a negligent and sluggish fellow, this idle custom ought certainly
to be avoided; being (as was observed) disagreeable to
the sight, offensive to the ear, and contrary also to that
natural claim which every one has to respect. For when
we indulge ourselves in this listless behaviour, we not
only intimate that the company we are in does not greatly please us, but also make a discovery not very advantageous to ourselves; I mean, that we are of a drowsy,
lethargic disposition, which must render us by no means
amiable or pleasing to those with whom we have converse.—Gellic.

A 2

were to think of a minuet, I am apt to believe that he would make a very poor mathematician.

There is time enough for every thing in the course of the day, if you do but one thing at once: but there is not time enough in the year, if you will do two things at a time.

This steady and undissipated attention to one object is a sure mark of a superior genius; as hurry, bustle, and agitation, are the never-failing symptoms of a weak and frivolous mind.

Indeed, without attention, nothing is to be done: want of attention, which is really want of thought, is either folly or madness. You should not only have attention to every thing, but a quickness of attention, so as to observe at once all the people in the room, their motions, their looks, and their words; and yet without staring at them, and seeming to be an observer. This quick and unobserved observation is of infinite advantage in life, and is to be acquired with care; and, on the contrary, what is called absence, which is a thoughtlessness and want of attention about what is doing, makes a man so like either a fool or madman, that, for my part, I see no real difference. A fool never has thought; a madman has lost it; and an absent man is, for the time, without it.

In short, the most material knowledge of all, I mean the knowledge of the world, is never to be acquired without great attention; and I know many old people, who, though they have lived long in the world, are but children still as to the knowledge of it, from their levity and inattention. Certain forms, which all people comply with, and certain arts, which all people aim at, hide in some degree the truth, and give a general exterior resemblance to

almost every body. Attention and sagacity must
see through that veil, and discover the natural character.

Add to this, there are little attentions which are
infinitely engaging, and which sensibly affect that
degree of pride and self-love which is inseparable
from human nature; as they are unquestionable
proofs of the regard and consideration which we
have for the persons to whom we pay them. As
for example: Suppose you invited any body to
dine or sup with you, you ought to recollect if you
had observed that they had any favourite dish, and
take care to provide it for them : and when it came,
you should say, ‘ You seemed to me, at such and
such a place, to give this dish a preference, and
therefore I ordered it. This is the wine that I observed you liked, and therefore I procured some.’—
Again; Most people have their weaknesses: they
have their aversions or their likings to such or such
things. If we were to laugh at a man for his aversion to a cat or cheese (which are common antipathies,) or by inattention or negligence to let them
come in his way, where we could prevent it, he
would, in the first case, think himself insulted, and,
in the second, slighted; and would remember both.
But, on the other hand, our care to procure for him
what he likes, and to remove from him what he dislikes, shows him that he is at least an object of our
attention, flatters his vanity, and perhaps makes
him more your friend than a more important service would have done. The more trifling these
things are, the more they prove your attention for
the person, and are consequently the more engaging.
Consult your own breast, and recollect how these
little attentions, when shown you by others, flatter

that degree of self-love and vanity, from which no man living is free. Reflect how they incline and attract you to that person, and how you are propitiated afterward to all which that person says or does. The same causes will have the same effect in your favour.

AWKWARDNESS OF DIFFERENT KINDS.

Many very worthy and sensible people have certain odd tricks, ill habits, and awkwardness in their behaviour,* which excite a disgust to and dislike of

---

* A gentleman ought not to run or walk in too great a hurry along the streets; for it is beneath the dignity of a person of any rank, and more becoming a running footman or a post-boy; besides that, in running, a man appears fatigued, perspires freely, and puffs and blows; all which are misbecoming a man of any consequence.

Nor yet ought our pace to be so very slow and tortoise-like, nor so stately and affected, like that of some lady of quality or a bride.

To stagger, likewise, or to totter about as we walk, and to stretch ourselves out, as it were, with monstrous strides, is foolish and ridiculous.

Neither ought your hands to hang dangling down; nor yet your arms to be projected or tossed backwards and forwards, like a ploughman that is sowing his corn.

Neither should you stare a man in the face when you meet, with your eyes fixed upon him, as if you saw something to wonder at in his appearance.

There are some people, likewise, who walk like a timorous or blind horse, lifting up their leg so high, as if they were drawing them out of a bushel; and some who stamp their feet with great violence against the ground, and with a noise hardly exceeded by the rumbling of a wagon. One man throws his feet out obliquely, as if he were kicking at you; this man knocks one knee against the other, or, perhaps, stoops down at every step to pull

their persons, that cannot be removed or overcome by any other valuable endowment or merit which they may possess.

Now, awkwardness can proceed but from two causes: either from not having kept good company, or from not having attended to it.

---

up his stockings. There are some who, by an indecent motion of their rumps, have an unequal kind of gait like the waddling of a duck; all which things, though not of much consequence, yet, being somewhat awkward and ungenteel, usually displease.

There are others who have a habit of distending their jaws every moment, twisting in their eyes, inflating their cheeks, puffing, blowing, and many other inelegant ways of disfiguring their faces; from which, if they at all studied what was becoming, they would entirely abstain. For Pallas herself, as the poets feign, used sometimes to amuse herself with playing upon the pipe, in which she was arrived at no common degree of excellence: but as she was one day very intent upon her amusement, she strolled to a fountain, where, surveying herself in the liquid mirror, and observing the strange and monstrous appearance of her countenance, she blushed, and immediately threw away her pipe; nor indeed without very good reason; for these kind of wind-instruments are not fit for a lady, nor indeed for a gentleman, but for the lower sort of people; who, through necessity, are obliged to practise it as a profession.

What is here said of this inelegant distortion of the face, is applicable to every other part of the human body. It is ungenteel to be continually thrusting out your tongue, or stroking up your beard, as many do; to smack your fingers or rub your hands; 'to elaborate a sigh' with a peculiarly doleful sound (like people in a fever,) which many people are guilty of; or to affect a sudden shivering over your whole body; or to bawl out when you are gaping, like a country-fellow that has been sleeping in a hay-loft.—*Galatee.*

When an awkward fellow first comes into a room, it is highly probable that his sword gets between his legs and throws him down, or makes him stumble at least; when he has recovered this accident, he goes and places himself in the very place of the whole room where he should not; there he soon lets his hat fall down, and in taking it up again, throws down his cane; in recovering his cane his hat falls the second time; so that he is a quarter of an hour before he is in order again. If he drinks tea or coffee, he certainly scalds his mouth, and lets either the cup or the saucer fall, and spills the tea or coffee in his breeches. At dinner his awkwardness distinguishes itself particularly, as he has more to do; there he holds his knife, fork, and spoon, differently from other people; eats with his knife to the great danger of his mouth, picks his teeth with his fork, and puts his spoon, which has been in his throat twenty times, into the dishes again. If he is to carve, he can never hit the joint; but in his vain efforts to cut through the bone, scatters the sauce in every body's face. He generally daubs himself with soup and grease, though his napkin is commonly stuck through a button-hole, and tickles his chin. When he drinks, he infallibly coughs in his glass, and besprinkles the company. Besides all this, he has strange tricks and gestures; such as snuffing up his nose, making faces, putting his fingers in his nose, or blowing it and looking afterward in his handkerchief, so as to make the company sick. His hands are troublesome to him when he has not something in them, and he does not know where to put them; but they are in perpetual motion between his bosom and his breeches;* he does not wear his clothes, and, in short, does nothing, like other people. All this, I own, is not in any degree criminal: but it is highly disagreeable and ridiculous in company, and ought most carefully to be avoided by whoever desires to please.

From this account of what you should not do, you may easily judge what you should do: and a due attention to the manners of people of fashion,

---

* The habit which some people have got, of thrusting their hands into their bosoms, or handling any part of their persons which is usually covered, is an obvious instance of indecency, and very improper.

In like manner, it is very unbecoming a well-bred man, and a gentleman, to make any sort of preparation, in the presence of others, for complying with the necessities of nature; and much more so to return to his company before he has completely adjusted every part of his dress.

There is a set of people extremely odious and troublesome, who in their conversation with others, by their gestures and behaviour, are really guilty of a lie; for though, by the confession of every one, the first, or at least a more honourable, place is justly due to them, yet they perpetually seize upon the very lowest; and it is an intolerable plague to force them up higher; for, like a startlish or refractory horse, they are every moment running back; so that, in a genteel company, there is an infinite deal of trouble with such people, whenever they come to a door; for they will by no means in the world be prevailed upon to go first, but run, sometimes across you, sometimes quite backwards, and with their hands and arms defend themselves, and make such a bustle, that at every third stair you must enter into a regular contest with them; by which means all the pleasure of your visit, or sometimes even the most important business, must be necessarily interrupted.— *Galateo.*

and who have seen the world, will make it habitual and familiar to you.

There is, likewise, an awkwardness of expression and words most carefully to be avoided; such as false English, bad pronunciation, old sayings, and common proverbs; which are so many proofs of having kept bad and low company. For example: If, instead of saying that 'tastes are different, and that every man has his own peculiar one,' you should let off a proverb, and say, that 'What is one man's meat is another man's poison;' or else, 'Every one as they like, as the good man said when he kissed his cow;' every body would be persuaded that you had never kept company with any body above footmen and housemaids.

There is likewise an awkwardness of the mind that ought to be, and with care may be, avoided: as, for instance, to mistake or forget names. To speak of Mr. What-d'ye call Him, or Mrs. Thingum, or How-d'ye-call Her, is excessively awkward and ordinary. To call people by improper titles, and appellations is so too; as My Lord, for Sir; and Sir for my Lord. To begin a story or narration when you are not perfect in it, and cannot go through with it, but are forced, possibly, to say in the middle of it, 'I have forgot the rest,' is very unpleasant and bungling. One must be extremely exact, clear, and perspicuous, in every thing one says; otherwise, instead of entertaining or informing others, one only tires and puzzles them.

BASHFULNESS.

BASHFULNESS is the distinguishing character of an English booby, who appears frightened out of his wits if people of fashion speak to him, and blushes and stammers without being able to give a proper answer; by which means he becomes truly ridiculous, from the groundless fear of being laughed at.

There is a very material difference between modesty and an awkward bashfulness, which is as ridiculous as true modesty is commendable: it is as absurd to be a simpleton as to be an impudent fellow; and we make ourselves contemptible if we cannot come into a room and speak to people without being out of countenance, or without embarrassment. A man who is really diffident, timid, and bashful, be his merit what it will, never can push himself in the world; his despondency throws him into inaction, and the forward, the bustling, and the petulant, will always precede him. The manner makes the whole difference. What would be impudence in one man, is only a proper and decent assurance in another. A man of sense, and of knowledge of the world, will assert his own rights and pursue his own objects, as steadily and intrepidly as the most impudent man living, and commonly more so; but then he has art enough to give an outward air of modesty to all he does. This engages and prevails, whilst the very same things shock and fail, from the overbearing or impudent manner only of doing them.

Englishmen, in general, are ashamed of going into company. When we avoid singularity, what should we be ashamed of? And why should not we go into a mixed company with as much ease, and as little concern, as we would go into our own room? Vice and ignorance are the only things we ought to be ashamed of: while we keep clear of them, we may venture any where without fear or concern. Nothing sinks a young man into low company so surely as bashfulness. If he thinks that he shall not, he must surely will not, please.

Some, indeed, from feeling the pain and inconveniencies of bashfulness, have rushed into the other extreme, and turned impudent; as cowards sometimes grow desperate from excess of danger: but this is equally to be avoided, there being nothing more generally shocking than impudence. The medium between these two extremes points out the well-bred man, who always feels himself firm and easy in all companies; who is modest without being bashful, and steady without being impudent.

A mean fellow is ashamed and embarrassed when he comes into company, is disconcerted when spoken to, answers with difficulty, and does not know how to dispose of his hands: but a gentleman who is acquainted with the world appears in company with a graceful and proper assurance, and is perfectly easy and unembarrassed. He is not dazzled by superior rank; he pays all the respect that is due to it, without being disconcerted; and can converse as easily with a king as with any one of his subjects. This is the great advantage of being introduced young into good company, and of conversing with our superiors. A well-bred man will converse with his inferiors without insolence, and with his superiors with respect and with ease. Add to this, that a man of a gentleman-like behaviour, though of inferior parts, is better received than a man of superior abilities, who is unacquainted with the world. Modesty and a polite easy assurance should be united.

COMPANY.

TO keep good company, especially at our first setting out, is the way to receive good impressions. Good company is not what respective sets of company are pleased either to call or think themselves. It consists chiefly (though not wholly) of people of considerable birth, rank, and character; for people of neither birth nor rank are frequently and very justly admitted into it, if distinguished by any peculiar merit, or eminency in any liberal art or science. So motley a thing is good company, that many people, without birth, rank, or merit, intrude into it by their own forwardness, and others get into it by the protection of some considerable person. In this fashionable good company the best manners and the purest language are most unquestionably to be learned; for they establish and give the Ton to both, which are called the language and manners of good company, neither of them being ascertained by any legal tribunal.

A company of people of the first quality cannot be called good company, in the common acceptation of the phrase, unless they are the fashionable and accredited company of the place; for people of the first quality can be as silly, as ill-bred, and as worthless, as people of the meanest degree. And a company consisting wholly of people of very low condition, whatever their merit or talents may be, can never be called good company; and therefore should not be much frequented, though by no means despised.

A company wholly composed of learned men, though greatly to be respected, is not meant by the words *good company:* they cannot have the easy and polished manners of the world, as they do not live in it. If we can bear our parts well in such a company, it will be proper to be in it sometimes, and we shall be more esteemed in other companies for having a place in that.

A company consisting wholly of professed wits and poets, is very inviting to young men who are pleased with it, if they have wit themselves; and, if they have none, are foolishly proud of being one of it. But such companies should be frequented with moderation and judgment. A wit is a very unpopular denomination, as it carries terror along with it; and people are as much afraid of a wit in company, as a woman is of a gun, which she supposes may go off of itself and do her a mischief. Their acquaintance, however, is worth seeking, and their company worth frequenting; but not exclusively of others, nor to such a degree as to be considered only as one of that particular set.

Above all things, endeavour to keep company with people above you; for there you rise, as much as you sink with people below you. When I say company above you, I do not mean with regard to their birth, but with regard to their merit, and the light in which the world considers them.

There are two sorts of good company: one, which is called the *Beau monde*, and consists of those people who have the lead in courts, and in the gay part of life; the other consists of those who are distinguished by some peculiar merit, or who excel in some particular or valuable art or science.

Be equally careful to avoid the low company, which in every sense of the word, is low indeed; low in rank, low in parts, low in manners, and low in merit. Vanity, that source of many of our fol

lies, and some of our crimes, has sunk many a man
into company in every light infinitely below him,
for the sake of being the first man in it. There he
dic/ates, is applauded and admired; but he soon
disgraces himself, and disqualifies himself for any
better company.

Having thus pointed out what company you
should avoid, and what company you should asso-
ciate with, I shall next lay down a few

*Cautions to be observed in adopting the manners of
a company.*

When a young man, new in the world, first gets
into company, he determines to conform to and
imitate it : but he too often mistakes the object of
his imitation. He has frequently heard the absurd
term of genteel and fashionable vices. He there
observes some people who shine, and who in general are admired and esteemed; and perceives that
these people are rakes, drunkards, or gamesters;
he therefore adopts their vices, mistaking their defects for their perfections, and imagining that they
owe their fashion and their lustre to these genteel
vices. But it is exactly the reverse; for these people have acquired their reputation by their parts,
their learning, their good-breeding, and other real
accomplishments; and are only blemished and
lowered in the opinions of all reasonable people by
these general and fashionable vices. It is therefore
plain that, in these mixed characters, the good part
only makes people forgive, but not approve, the
bad.

If a man should unfortunately have any vices,
he ought at least to be content with his own, and

not adopt other people's. The adoption of vice
has ruined ten times more young men, than natural
inclinations.

Let us imitate the real perfections of the good
company into which we may get; copy their politeness, their carriage, their address, and their easy
and well-bred turn of their conversation; but we
should remember, that, let them shine ever so bright,
their vices, if they have any, are so many blemishes,
which we should no more endeavour to imitate than
we would make artificial warts upon our faces because some very handsome men had the misfortune to have a natural one upon his. We should,
on the contrary, think how much handsomer he
would have been without it.

Having thus given you instructions for making
you well received in good company,* I proceed

Rules for behaviour in company.

Nothing ought to be said or done which may by any
means discover, that those whose company we are in are
not much beloved, or, at least, much esteemed by us.

It should seem, therefore, not a very decent custom
(which yet is practised by some people,) to affect to be
drowsy, and even fall asleep (on purpose as it were,)
where a genteel company is met together for their mutual entertainment: for, certainly, those that behave in
this manner declare, in effect, tha. they do not much esteem those who are present, or pay any regard to their
conversation; not to mention, that something may happen in their sleep, (especially if they are any ways in-
disposed) that may be disagreeable either to the eyes or
the ears of the company: for one often sees in such sleepy
folks the sweat run down their faces, or their saliva down
their beards, in no very decent manner.

For the same reason, it is rather a troublesome prac-

next to lay before you, what you will find of equal
use and importance in your commerce with the
world, some directions, or

RULES FOR CONVERSATION.

Talking.

WHEN you are in company, talk often, but ne-

tice for any one to rise up in an assembly thus conversing
together, and to walk about the room.

You meet with some people, likewise, who are continually wriggling and twisting themselves about; stretch-
ing and gaping, and turning themselves sometimes on one
side, sometimes on another, as if they were seized with
a sudden fever; which is a certain indication that they
are tired and disgusted with their present company.

In like manner, they act very improperly who pull out
of their pockets first one letter, then another, and read
them before the company.

And much worse does he behave, who, taking out his
scissors or his penknife, sets himself, with great composure, to cut and polish his nails; as if he had an utter
contempt for those that are present, and therefore, to deceive the time, was endeavouring to amuse himself in
some other manner.

We ought also carefully to abstain from those little
ways which are much in use, of humming a tune to ourselves, imitating the beating of a drum with our fingers
upon a table, or kicking out our feet alternately in an in-
solent manner; for these are all indications of our contempt for others.

Moreover, it is by no means decent to sit in such a
manner as either to turn our backs upon any part of the
company, or to lift up our legs so as to discover to the
eyes of others those parts of the body which are usually
concealed; for we never act thus but in the presence of
those for whose good opinion we have not the least
regard.—*Galatee*

ver long; in that case, if you do not please, at least you are sure not to tire your hearers.*

* There are many persons who never know when to leave off prating; and, like a ship which, once put in motion by the force of the winds, even when the sails are furled, will not stop,—so these loquacious people, being carried on by a certain impulse, continue their career; and though they have nothing to talk of, they nevertheless proceed; and either inculcate over and over again what they have already said, or utter at random whatever comes uppermost.

There are also some people who labour under so great and insatiable an appetite for talking, that they will interrupt others when they are going to speak; and as we sometimes see, on a farmer's dunghill in the country, young chickens snatching grains of corn out of each other's little bills, so these people catch up the discourse out of the mouth of another, who has begun speaking, and immediately hold forth themselves; which is so provoking to some people, that they would rather interchange blows than words with them, and rather fight than converse with them; for, if you accurately observe the humours of mankind, there is nothing which sooner, or more certainly, provokes a man, than the giving a sudden check to his desires and inclinations, even in the most trifling affair.

Now, as an immoderate loquacity, or love of talking, gives disgust, so too great a taciturnity, or an affected silence, is very disagreeable: for to observe a haughty silence, where others take their turn in the conversation, seems to be nothing else than unwillingness to contribute your share to the common entertainment: and as to speak is to open your mind, as it were, to those that hear you, he, on the contrary, who is entirely silent, seems to shun all acquaintance with the rest of the company. Wherefore, as these people who, at their entertainments on any joyful occasion, drink freely, and perhaps get drunk, love to get rid of people who will not drink, so no one desires

*Learn the characters of the company before you
talk much.*

Inform yourself of the characters and situations
of the company before you give way to what your
imagination may prompt you to say. There are
in all companies more wrong heads than right ones,
and many more who deserve, than who like, censure. Should you therefore expatiate in the praise
of some virtue, which some in company notoriously
want, or declaim against any vice which others are
notoriously infected with, your reflections, however
general and unapplied, will, by being applicable, be
thought personal, and levelled at those people.
This consideration points out to you sufficiently not
to be suspicious and captious yourself, nor to suppose that things, because they may, are therefore
meant at, you.

Telling stories and digressions.

Tell stories very seldom, and absolutely never
but where they are very apt, and very short. Omit
every circumstance that is not material, and beware
of digressions. To have frequent recourse to narrative, betrays great want of imagination.*

---

to see these silent gentry in their cheerful, friendly meet-
ings: the most agreeable society, therefore, is that where
every one is at liberty to speak or keep silence in his
turn.—*Galateo.*

* If you have a mind to relate any thing in company,
it is proper, before you begin, to have the whole story,
whether a piece of history or any late occurrence, well
settled in your mind; as also, every name and expression ready at hand, that you may not be obliged every

B

Seizing people by the button.

Never hold any body by the button, or the hand, in order to be heard out; for if people are not will-

---

moment to interrupt your narration, and inquire of other people, and beg their assistance; sometimes in regard to the fact itself. sometimes the names of persons, and other circumstances, of what you have undertaken to recite.

But, if you are to relate any thing which was said or done amongst any number of people, you ought not too frequently to use the expressions of—'He said,' or 'He replied;' because these pronouns agree equally with all the persons concerned; and this ambiguity must necessarily lead the audience into an error. It is proper therefore that he who relates any fact should make use of some proper names, and take care not to change them one for another during the narration.

Moreover, the reciter of any incident ought to avoid the mentioning those circumstances, which, if omitted, the story would not be less, or rather, would be more agreeable without them.   'The person I speak of was son of Mr. Such-a-one, who lives in St. James-street, do you know the man? His wife was daughter to Mr. Such-a-one, she was a thin woman, who used to come constantly to prayers at St. Lawrence's church: you must certainly know her.—Zounds! if you do not know her, you know nothing!' Or, 'He was a handsome, tall old gentleman, who wore his own long hair. do not you recollect him?'—Now, if the very same thing might as well have happened to any other person which happened to him, all this long disquisition were to little purpose; nay, must be very tedious and provoking to the audience, who being impatient to arrive at a complete knowledge of the affair which you have begun upon, you seem de termined to delay the gratifying their curiosity as long as possible.—*Galateo.*

ing to hear you, you had much better hold your
tongue than they.*

Long talkers and whisperers.

Long talkers generally single out some unfortunate man in company to whisper, or at least, in a
half voice, to convey a continuity of words to. This
is excessively ill-bred, and, in some degree, a fraud;
conversation-stock being a joint and common property. But if one of these unmerciful talkers lays
hold of you, hear him with patience, (and at least
with seeming attention,) if he is worth obliging;
for nothing will oblige him more than a patient hearing, as nothing would hurt him more, than either to
leave him in the midst of his discourse, or to discover your impatience under your affliction.

Inattention to persons speaking.

There is nothing so brutally shocking, nor so little forgiven, as a seeming inattention to the person
who is speaking to you;† and I have known many
a man knocked down for a much slighter provocation than that inattention which I mean. I have

---

*When you are talking to any one, do not be conti-
nually punching him in the side, as some people are
who, after every sentence, keep asking the person they
are conversing with, 'Did not I tell you so?' 'What do
you think of the matter?' 'What say you, sir?' and in
the mean time they are every moment jogging and
thrusting him with their elbow; which cannot be considered as a mark of respect.—*Galateo.*

† It is also a very disagreeable practice to interrupt a
person by any noise in the midst of his speech; which,
indeed, must give the person interrupted much the same
pleasure as it would give you, if, when you were just

seen many people, who, while you are speaking to
them, instead of looking at and attending to you,
fix their eyes upon the ceiling, or some other part
of the room, look out of the window, play with a
dog, twirl their snuff-box, or pick their nose. Nothing discovers a little, futile, frivolous mind more
than this, and nothing is so offensively ill-bred; it
is an explicit declaration on your part, that every
the most trifling object deserves your attention more
than all that can be said by the person who is speak-

---

reaching the goal in full speed, any one should suddenly
draw you back.

Neither is it consistent with good manners, when another person is speaking, that you should contrive, either
by showing something new, or by calling the attention
of the company another way, to make him neglected and
forsaken by his audience.

Neither does it become you to dismiss the company,
who were not invited by you, but by some other person.

You ought also to be attentive, when any one is talking to you, that you may not be under the necessity of
asking every moment, ‘What do you say?’ ‘How did
you say?’ under which fault, indeed, many people labour; when yet this is not attended with less trouble to
the speaker than if, in walking, he were every moment
to kick his foot against a stone. All these practices, and,
in general, whatever may check the speaker in his course,
whether directly or obliquely, are carefully to be avoided.

And if any one be somewhat slow in speaking, you
ought not to forestall him, or supply him with proper
words, as if you alone were rich and he were poor in expressions; for many people are apt to take this ill, those
especially who have an opinion of their own eloquence;
and therefore they think you do not pay them that deference which they imagine to be their due, and that you
are desirous of suggesting hints to them in that art, in
which they fancy themselves great proficients.— *Galateo.*

ing to you. Judge of the sentiments of hatred and resentment which such treatment must excite in every breast where any degree of self-love dwells. I repeat it again and again, that sort of vanity and self-love is inseparable from human nature, whatever may be its rank or condition; even your footman will sooner forget and forgive a beating, than any manifest mark of slight and contempt. Be, therefore, not only really, but seemingly and manifestly, attentive to whoever speaks to you.

Never interrupt any speaker.

It is considered as the height of ill-manners to interrupt any person while speaking, by speaking yourself, or calling off the attention of the company to any new subject. This, however, every child knows.

Adopt rather than give the subject.

Take, rather than give, the subject of the company you are in. If you have parts, you will show them, more or less, upon every subject; and if you have not, you had better talk sillily upon a subject of other people's than of your own choosing.

Conceal your learning from the company.

Never display your learning, but on particular occasions. Reserve it for learned men, and let even these rather extort it from you than appear forward to display it. Hence you will be deemed modest, and reputed to possess more knowledge than you really have. Never seem wiser or more learned than your company. . The man who affects to display his learning, will be frequently questioned; and, if found superficial, will be ridiculed and despised; if otherwise, he will be deemed a pedant. Nothing can lessen real merit (which will always show itself) in the opinion of the world, but an ostentatious display of it by its possessor.

Contradict with politeness.

When you oppose or contradict any person's assertion or opinion, let your manner, your air, your terms, and your tone of voice be soft and gentle, and that easily and naturally, not affectedly. Use palliatives when you contradict; such as, 'I may be deceived—I am not sure, but I believe—I should rather think, &c.'* Finish any argument or dispute

---

* You ought to accustom yourself to an elegant, modest, and pleasing manner of expression; and such as hath nothing offensive to those you converse with. Thus, instead of saying, 'Sir, you do not understand me,' you ought rather to say, 'I believe I do not express myself so clearly as I ought to do.' It is also better to say, 'Let us consider the affair more accurately—whether we take it right or not,' than 'You mistake, or 'It is not so;' or 'You know nothing of the matter;' for it is a polite and amiable practice to make some excuse for another, even in those instances where you are convinced he might justly be blamed; nay, though your friend alone has been in a mistake, yet you should represent the mistake as common to you both; and when you have ascribed some part of it to yourself, then you may venture to admonish or to reprove him in some such expressions as these: 'We are under a very great mistake here; or 'We did not recollect how we settled this affair yesterday;' though, perhaps it was *he* alone, and not you, that was so forgetful.

That kind of expressions also, which rude people sometimes make use of, such as, 'If what you say is true,' is extremely unpolite; for a man's veracity ought not so very lightly to be called in question.

with some little good-humoured pleasantry, to show
that you are neither hurt yourself, nor meant to
hurt your antagonist ; for an argument, kept up
a good while, often occasions a temporary aliena-
tion on each side.

Avoid argument if possible.

Avoid, as much as you can, in mixed companies,
argumentative, polemical conversations, which certainly indispose, for a time, the contending parties
towards each other; and, if the controversy grows
warm and noisy, endeavour to put an end to it by
some genteel levity or joke.

Always debate with temper.

Arguments should never be maintained with heat
and clamour, though we believe or know ourselves
to be in the right : we should give our opinions modestly and coolly ; and, if that will not do, endea
vour to change the conversation by saying, 'We
shall not be able to convince one another, nor is it
necessary that we should; so let us talk of something else.'*

---

* Those people, likewise, who contradict whatever is
spoken by others, and make every assertion matter of dispute and altercation, discover by that very behaviour
that they are very little acquainted with human nature:
for every one is fond of victory ; and it is with extreme
reluctance that they submit to be overborne, either in
conversation or in the management of affairs. Besides,
to be so ready to oppose other people, upon all occasions,
is conversing like enemies rather than friends : he, therefore, that wishes to appear amiable and agreeable to his
acquaintance, will not have continually in his mouth expressions of this kind : ''Tis false, sir: whatever you

Local propriety to be observed.

Remember that there is a local propriety to be observed in all companies; and that what is extremely proper in one company may be, and often is, highly improper in another.

Jokes, bons mots, &c.

The jokes, *bons mots*, the little adventures, which may do very well in one company, will seem flat and tedious when related in another. The particular characters, the habits, the cant, of one company may give merit to a word or a gesture, which would have none at all if divested of those accidental circumstances. Here people very commonly err; and fond of something that has entertained them in one company, and in certain circumstan-

---

may think, the affair is as I say;' and the like. Nor let him be so ready to prove every trifle by a bet or wager; but rather let him make it a constant rule to submit with complaisance to the opinion of others, especially in matters of no great moment; because victories of this kind often cost a man extremely dear; for he that comes off victorious in some frivolous dispute, frequently suffers the loss of some intimate friend; and at the same time makes himself so disagreeable to others, that they dare not venture to be upon a familiar footing with him, for fear of being every moment engaged in some foolish altercation.

If any one, however, should at any time be drawn into a dispute by the company he is engaged in, let him manage it in a mild and gentle manner, and not appear too eager for the victory; but let every one so far enjoy his own opinion, as to leave the decision of the matter in question to the majority, or at least to the most zealous part of the company; and thus the victory, as due, will voluntarily be yielded to you.—*Galateo.*

ces, repeat it with emphasis in another, where it is either insipid, or it may be offensive, by being ill-timed or misplaced. Nay, they often do it with this silly preamble: 'I will tell you an excellent thing;' or, 'I will tell you the best thing in the world.' This raises expectations, which, when absolutely disappointed, make the relator of this excellent thing look very deservedly like a fool.

Egotism.

Upon all occasions avoid speaking of yourself, if it be possible. Some abruptly speak advantageously of themselves, without either pretence or provocation. This is downright impudence.—Others proceed more artfully, as they imagine; forging accusations against themselves, and complaining of calumnies which they never heard, in order to justify themselves, and exhibit a catalogue of their many virtues. 'They acknowledge, indeed, it may appear odd that they should talk thus of themselves; it is what they have a great aversion to, and what they could not have done if they had not been thus unjustly and scandalously abused.' This thin veil of modesty, drawn before vanity, is much too transparent to conceal it, even from those who have but a moderate share of penetration.

Others go to work more modestly and more slily still; they confess themselves guilty of all the cardinal virtues, by first degrading them into weaknesses, and then acknowledging their misfortune in being made up of those weaknesses. 'They cannot see people labouring under misfortunes, without sympathizing with and endeavouring to help them. They cannot see their fellow-creatures in distress, without relieving them; though, truly, their cir-

B 2

cumstances cannot very well afford it. They cannot avoid speaking the truth, though they acknowledge it to be sometimes imprudent. In short, they confess that, with all these weaknesses, they are not fit to live in the world, much less to prosper in it. But they are now too old to pursue a contrary conduct, and therefore they must rub on as well as they can.'

Though this may appear too ridiculous and *outre* even for the stage, yet it is frequently met with upon the common stage of the world. This principle of vanity and pride is so strong in human nature, that it descends even to the lowest objects; and we often see people fishing for praise, where, admitting all they say to be true, no just praise is to be caught. One perhaps affirms that he has rode post a hundred miles in six hours: probably this is a falsehood: but, even supposing it to be true; what then? Why it must be admitted that he is a very good post-boy, that is all. Another asserts, perhaps not without a few oaths, that he has drunk six or eight bottles of wine at a sitting. It would be charitable to believe such a man a liar; for, if we do not, we must certainly pronounce him a beast.

There are a thousand such follies and extravagancies which vanity draws people into, and which always defeat their own purpose. The only method of avoiding these evils, is never to speak of ourselves: but when in a narrative, we are obliged to mention ourselves, we should take care not to drop a single word that can directly or indirectly be construed as fishing for applause. Be our characters what they will they will be known; and nobody will take them upon our own words. Nothing that we can say ourselves will varnish our defects, or add lustre to our perfections; but, on the contrary, it will often make the former more glaring, and the latter obscure. If we are silent upon our own merits, neither envy, indignation, nor ridicule, will obstruct or allay the applause which we may really deserve. But if we are our own panegyrists upon any occasion, however artfully dressed or disguised, every one will conspire against us, and we shall be disappointed of the very end we aim at.*

Be not dark nor mysterious.

Take care never to seem dark and mysterious;

* Neither ought any one to boast of his nobility, his honours, or his riches, much less of his own wisdom; or magnificently to extol the bravery and great actions, either of himself or of his ancestors; or, what is but too common, at every other word, to talk of his family : for, he that does thus will appear to do it in opposition to the present company, especially if they are not, or at least think they are not less noble, less honourable, or less brave than himself. Or, if they are really his inferiors in rank or station, he will be deemed to oppress them, as it were, by his grandeur, and designedly to reproach them with their meanness and misery; which must be universally displeasing to all mankind.

Nor yet ought any one to extenuate or demean himself too much, any more than he should immoderately exalt himself, but rather subtract a little from his real dignity and merits, than arrogate too much by his words, even in the most trifling instance. For what is really laudable must displease in the excess.

Yet, it must be observed, that those who immoderately extenuate their actions by their words, and renounce those honours which are indisputably their due, by that very conduct discover a greater degree of pride, even than those who, in this respect, usurp what does not belong to them.—*Galateo.*

which is not only a very unamiable character, but a very suspicious one too: if you seem mysterious with others, they will be really so with you, and you will know nothing. The height of abilities is to have a frank, open, and ingenuous exterior, with a prudent and reserved interior; to be upon your own guard, and yet, by a seeming natural openness, to put people off of theirs. The majority of every company will avail themselves of every indiscreet and unguarded expression of yours, if they can turn it to their own advantage.

Look people in the face when speaking.

Always look people in the face when you speak to them: the not doing it is thought to imply conscious guilt; besides that, you lose the advantage of observing, by their countenances, what impression your discourse makes upon them. In order to know people's real sentiments, I trust much more to my eyes than to my ears; for they can say whatever they have a mind I should hear, but they can seldom help looking what they have no intention that I should know.

Scandal.

Private scandal should never be received nor retailed willingly; for though the defamation of others may, for the present, gratify the malignity or the pride of our hearts, yet cool reflection will draw very disadvantageous conclusions from such a disposition. In scandal, as in robbery, the receiver is always thought as bad as the thief.*

---

* We ought not to speak slightly of others, or of their affairs; for, notwithstanding we may seem by that means

Never indulge general reflections

Never, in conversation, attack whole bodies of any kind; for you may thereby unnecessarily make yourself a great number of enemies. Among women, as among men, there are good as well as bad, and, it may be, full as many, or more good than among men. This rule holds as to lawyers, soldiers, parsons, courtiers, citizens, &c. They are all men, subject to the same passions and sentiments, differing only in the manner, according to their several educations; and it would be as imprudent as unjust to attack any of them by the lump. Individuals forgive sometimes, but bodies and societies never do. Many young people think it very genteel and witty to abuse the clergy; in which they are extremely deceived; since, in my opinion, parsons are very like men, and neither the better nor the worse for wearing a black gown. All general reflections upon nations and societies are the trite threadbare jokes of those who set up for wit without having any, and so have recourse to common-place. Judge of individuals from your own knowledge of them, and not from their sex, profession, or denomination.

Mimicry.

Mimicry, which is the common and favourite

---

so gain the most willing and ready attention (from the envy which mankind usually conceive at the advantages and honours which are paid to others,) yet every one will at length avoid us, as they would a mischievous bull; for all men shun the acquaintance of people addicted to scandal; naturally supposing that what they say of others in their company, they will say of them in the company of others.—*Galateo.*

amusement of little, low minds, is in the utmost
contempt with great ones. It is the lowest and
most illiberal of all buffoonery. We should neither
practise it, nor applaud it in others. Besides that
the person mimicked is insulted; and, as I have
often observed to you before, an insult is never forgiven.*

Swearing.

We may frequently hear some people, in good
company, interlard their conversation with oaths,

---

* Neither ought any thing to be done in an abject, fawn
ing, or buffoonish manner, merely to make other people
laugh; such as distorting our mouths or our eyes, and imitating the follies and gesticulations of a harlequin or a mer-
ry-andrew: for no one ought basely to demean himself
to please other people. This is not the accomplishment
of a gentleman, but of a mimic and a buffoon; whose
vulgar and plebeian methods of entertaining their company ought by no means to be imitated.

Yet I would not have you affect a stupid insensibility
in this respect, or too great delicacy on these occasions;
but he that can seasonably produce something new and
smart (in this way,) and not obvious to every one, let him
produce it; but he that is not blest with this faculty, let
him hold his tongue; for these things proceed from the
different turn of men's minds; which, if they are elegant
and agreeable, they convey an idea (the ingenuity and
readiness of wit in the person that utters them, which
generally gives great pleasure to others, and renders the
person agreeable and entertaining; but, if the contrary
is the case, we must expect a contrary effect; for people that aim at this kind of wit, without the ability, are like
an ass that pretends to be pleasant, or a fat, punch-bellied
fellow, who should attempt to lead up a minuet, or strip
himself and dance a hornpipe upon the stage.—*Galateo*

by way of embellishment, as they suppose; but we must observe, too, that those who do so are never those who contribute in any degree to give that company the denomination of good company. They are generally people of low education; for swearing, without having a single temptation to plead, is as silly, and as illiberal, as it is wicked.

Sneering.

Whatever we say in company, if we say it with a supercilious, cynical face, or an embarrassed countenance, or a silly, disconcerted grin, it will be ill received. If we mutter it, or utter it indistinctly and ungracefully, it will be still worse received.*

Talk not of your own nor other person's private affairs.

Never talk of your own or other people's domestic affairs; yours are nothing to them, but tedious; theirs are nothing to you. It is a tender subject, and it is a chance if you do not touch somebody or other's sore place. In this case there is no trusting to specious appearances, which are often so contrary to the real situation of things between men and their wives, parents and their children, seeming friends, &c. that, with the best intentions in the world, we very often make some very disagreeable blunders.†

---

* He also, who, either in token of admiration, or by way of sneer, makes a particular kind of noise with his mouth, exhibits an idea of deformity; and these things, which are thus expressed by signs, differ but little from the things themselves.

† A great part of mankind are so wonderfully pleased with themselves, as not in the least to regard whether

Explicitness.

Nothing makes a man look sillier in company, than a joke or pleasantry not relished or not understood; and, if he meets with a profound silence when he expected a general applause; or, what is

---

they please or displease other people; and, in order to display their own sagacity, great sense and wisdom, they will be giving their advice to one man, finding fault with another, and disputing with a third; and, in short, they oppose the opinions of other people with so much vehemence, that from words they often come to blows, as they will allow no weight in any one's opinion but their own. But to give one's advice to others, unasked, is in effect to declare that we are much wiser than those to whom we give it, and is a kind of reproaching them with their ignorance and inexperience. This freedom, therefore, ought not to be taken with mere common acquaintance, but only with those to whom we are united by the most intimate friendship, or those of whom the care and inspection is particularly committed to our charge; or even with a stranger, if we perceive him to be threatened with any imminent danger. But in our daily intercourse with mankind, we ought to be cautious not to obtrude our advice too officiously upon others, nor show ourselves impertinently solicitous about their affairs. Into this mistake, however, many are apt to fall, but for the most part people of no great depth of understanding; for those ignorant and superficial people are led merely by their senses, and seldom make any deep reflections upon what comes before them; being that sort of men who have scarcely any matters of consequence submitted to their disquisition and examination. But, however this may be, he that is offering his advice upon all occasions, and thus distributing it at random, gives a plain intimation to the rest of the world that they are entirely destitute of that wisdom and prudence in which he so greatly abounds. *Galateo.*

still worse, if he is desired to explain the joke or *bon mot;* his awkward and embarrassed situation is easier imagined than described.

Secrecy.

Be careful how you repeat in one company what you hear in another. Things seemingly indifferent may, by circulation, have much graver consequences than may be imagined. There is a kind of general tacit trust in conversation, by which a man is engaged not to report any thing out of it, though he is not immediately enjoined secrecy. A retailer of this kind draws himself into a thousand scrapes and discussions, and is shily and indifferently received wherever he goes.

Adapt your conversation to the company.

Always adapt your conversation to the people you are conversing with; for I suppose you would not talk upon the same subject, and in the same manner, to a bishop, a philosopher, a captain, and a woman.

Never suppose yourself the subject or laugh of the company.

People of an ordinary, low education, when they happen to fall into good company, imagine themselves the only object of its attention: if the company whispers, it is, to be sure, concerning them; if they laugh, it is at them; and if any thing ambiguous, that by the most forced interpretation can be applied to them, happens to be said, they are convinced that it was meant for them; upon which they grow out of countenance first, and then angry. This mistake is very well ridiculed in the Strata-

gem, where Scrub says, 'I am sure they talked of
me! for they laughed consumedly.' A well-bred
man seldom thinks, but never seems to think, himself slighted, undervalued, or laughed at in company, unless where it is so plainly marked out, that
his honour obliges him to resent it in a proper manner. On the contrary, a vulgar man is captious
and jealous; eager and impetuous about trifles.—
He suspects himself to be slighted; thinks every
thing that is said meant at him: if the company
happens to laugh, he is persuaded they laugh at
him; he grows angry and testy, says something
very impertinent, and draws himself into a scrape,
by showing what he calls a proper spirit, and as-
serting himself. The conversation of a vulgar man
also always savours strongly of the lowness of his
education and company. It turns chiefly upon his
domestic affairs, his servants, the excellent order
he keeps in his own family, and the little anecdotes
of the neighbourhood; all which he relates with
emphasis, as interesting matters. He is a man
gossip.

Seriousness.

A certain degree of exterior seriousness in looks
and motions gives dignity, without excluding wit
and decent cheerfulness. A constant smirk upon
the face, and a whiffling activity of the body, are
strong indications of futility.

ECONOMY.

A fool squanders away, without credit or advantage to himself, more than a man of sense
spends with both. The latter employs his money
as he does his time, and never spends a shilling of

the one, nor a minute of the other, but in something
that is either useful or rationally pleasing to himself
or others. The former buys whatever he does not
want, and does not pay for what he does want.—
He cannot withstand the charms of a toy-shop:
snuff boxes, watches, heads of canes, &c. are his
destruction. His servants and tradesmen conspire
with his own indolence to cheat him; and in a
very little time he is astonished, in the midst of all
these ridiculous superfluities, to find himself in want
of all the real comforts and necessaries of life.

Without care and method, the largest fortune will
not, and with them almost the smallest will, sup
ply all necessary expenses. As far as you can
possibly, pay ready money for every thing you buy,
and avoid bills. Pay that money too yourself, and
not through the hands of any servant; who always either stipulates poundage, or requires a present for his good words, as they call it. Where
you must have bills, (as for meat and drink, clothes,
&c.) pay them regularly every month, and with
your own hand. Never, from a mistaken economy,
buy a thing you do not want, because it is cheap;
or, from a silly pride, because it is dear. Keep an
account, in a book, of all that you receive, and of
all that you pay; for no man who knows what he
receives, and what he pays, ever runs out. I do
not mean that you should keep an account of the
shillings and half crowns which you may spend in
chair hire, &c. they are unworthy of the time and
the ink that they would consume; leave such *mi-
nutiæ* to dull, penny-wise fellows: but remember,
in economy, as in every other part of life, to have
the proper attention to proper objects, and the proper contempt for little ones.

FRIENDSHIP.

Young persons have commonly an unguarded frankness about them, which makes them the easy prey and bubbles of the artful and the experienced; they look upon every knave or fool who tells them that he is their friend, to be really so; and pay that profession of stimulated friendship with an indiscreet and unbounded confidence, always to their loss, often to their ruin. Beware of these proffered friendships. Receive them with great civility, but with great incredulity too; and pay them with compliments, but not with confidence. Do not suppose that people become friends at first sight, or even upon a short acquaintance. Real friendship is a slow grower; and never thrives unless ingrafted upon a stock of known and reciprocal merit.

There is another kind of nominal friendship among young people, which is warm for the time, but luckily of short duration. This friendship is hastily produced, by their being accidentally thrown together, and pursuing the same course of riot and debauchery. A fine friendship, truly! and well cemented by drunkenness and lewdness. It should rather be called a conspiracy against morals and good manners, and be punished as such by the civil magistrate. However, they have the impudence, and the folly, to call this confederacy a friendship. They lend one another money, for bad purposes; they engage in quarrels, offensive and defensive, for their accomplices; they tell one another all they know, and often more too: when, on a sudden, some accident disperses them, and they think no more of each other, unless it be to betray and laugh at their imprudent confidence.

When a man uses strong protestations or oaths to make you believe a thing, which is of itself so probable that the bare saying of it would be sufficient, depend upon it he deceives you, and is highly interested in making you believe it, or else he would not take so much pains.

Remember to make a great difference between companions and friends; for a very complaisant and agreeable companion may, and often does, prove a very improper and a very dangerous friend. People will, in a great degree, form their opinion of you, upon that which they have of your friends; and there is a Spanish proverb, which says, very justly, 'Tell me whom you live with, and I will tell you who you are.' One may fairly suppose, that a man who makes a knave, or a fool his friend, has something very bad to do or to conceal. But, at the same time that you carefully decline the friendship of knaves and fools, if it can be called friendship, there is no occasion to make either of them your enemies, wantonly and unprovoked; for they are numerous bodies; and I would rather choose a secure neutrality, than an alliance or war with either of them. You may be declared enemy to their vices and follies, without being marked out by them as a personal one. Their enmity is the next dangerous thing to their friendship. Have a real reserve with almost every body; and have a seeming reserve with almost nobody; for it is very disagreeable to seem reserved, and very dangerous not to be so. Few people find the true medium: many are ridiculously mysterious and reserved upon trifles; and many imprudently communicative of all they know.

GOOD BREEDING.

Good breeding has been very justly defined to be the result of much good sense, some good nature, and a little self-denial for the sake of others, and with a view to obtain the same indulgence from them.

Good breeding cannot be attended to too soon or too much; it must be acquired while young, or it is never quite easy; and, if it is acquired young, will always last and be habitual. Horace says, *Quo semel est imbuta recens, servabit odorem testa diu:* to show the advantage of giving young people good habits and impressions in their youth.

Good breeding alone can prepossess people in our favour at first sight; more time being necessary to discover greater talents. Good breeding, however, does not consist in low bows and formal ceremony; but in an easy, civil, and respectful behaviour.

Indeed, good sense in many cases must determine good breeding; for what will be civil at one time, and to one person, would be rude at another time, and to another person: there are, however, some general rules of good breeding. As for example: To answer only Yes, or No, to any person, without adding Sir, My Lord, or Madam, (as it may happen,) is always extremely rude; and it is equally so not to give proper attention and a civil answer when spoken to: such behaviour convinces the person who is speaking to us, that we despise him, and do not think him worthy of our attention or an answer.

A well bred person will take care to answer with complaisance when he is spoken to; will place him

self at the lower end of the table, unless bid to go
higher; will first drink to the lady of the house,
and then to the master; he will not eat awkwardly,
or dirtily, nor sit when others stand; and he will
do all this with an air of complaisance, and not
with a grave ill-natured look, as if he did it all unwillingly.

There is nothing more difficult to attain, or so
necessary to possess, as perfect good breeding,
which is equally inconsistent with a stiff formality,
an impertinent forwardness, and an awkward bashfulness. A little ceremony is sometimes necessary;
a certain degree of firmness is absolutely so; and
an outward modesty is extremely becoming.

Virtue and learning, like gold, have their intrin-
sic value; but if they are not polished, they certainly lose a great deal of their lustre: and even polished brass will pass upon more people than rough
gold. What a number of sins does the cheerful,
easy, good breeding of the French frequently cover!

My Lord Bacon says, 'That a pleasing figure is
a perpetual letter of recommendation.' It is certainly an agreeable forerunner of Merit, and smooths
the way for it.

A man of good breeding should be acquainted
with the forms and particular customs of courts.
At Vienna, men always make curtseys, instead of
bows, to the emperor: in France, nobody bows to
the king, or kisses his hand; but in Spain and England, bows are made, and hands are kissed. Thus
every court has some peculiarity, which those who
visit them ought previously to inform themselves
of, to avoid blunders and awkwardness.

Very few, scarcely any, are wanting in the respect which they should show to those whom they

acknowledge to be infinitely their superiors. The man of fashion, and of the world, expresses it in its fullest extent; but naturally, easily, and without concern; whereas a man who is not used to keep good company, expresses it awkwardly; one sees that he is not used to it, and that it costs him a great deal: but I never saw the worst bred man living guilty of lolling, whistling, scratching his head, and such like indecencies, in company that he respected. In such companies, therefore, the only point to be attended to is, to show that respect which every body means to show, in an easy, unembarrassed, and graceful manner.

In mixed companies, whoever is admitted to make part of them, is, for the time at least, supposed to be upon a footing of equality with the rest; and, consequently, every one claims, and very justly, every mark of civility and good breeding. Ease is allowed, but carelessness and negligence are strictly forbidden. If a man accosts you, and talks to you ever so dully or frivolously, it is worse than rudeness, it is brutality, to show him, by a manifest inattention to what he says, that you think him a fool or a blockhead, and not worth hearing. It is much worse so with regard to women; who, of whatever rank they are, are entitled, in consideration of their sex, not only to an attentive, but an officious, good breeding from men. Their little wants, likings, dislikes, preferences, antipathies, fancies, whims, and even impertinences, must be officiously attended to, flattered, and, if possible, guessed at and anticipated by a well-bred man. You must never usurp to yourself those conveniences and *agremens* which are of common right; such as the best places, the best

dishes, &c. but, on the contrary, always decline
them yourself, and offer them to others; who, in
their turns, will offer them to you: so that, upon
the whole, you will, in your turn, enjoy your share
of common right.

The third sort of good breeding is local, and is
variously modified in not only different countries,
but in different towns of the same country. But it
must be founded upon the two former sorts; they
are the matter, to which, in this case, fashion and
custom only give the different shapes and impressions. Whoever has the first two sorts will easily
acquire this third sort of good breeding, which depends singly upon attention and observation. It is
properly the polish, the lustre, the last finishing-
strokes of good breeding. A man of sense, therefore, carefully attends to the local manners of the
respective places where he is, and takes for his models those persons whom he observes to be at the
head of the fashion and good breeding. He watches
how they address themselves to their superiors,
how they accost their equals, and how they treat
their inferiors; and lets none of those little nice-
ties escape him, which are to good breeding what
the last delicate and masterly touches are to a good
picture, and which the vulgar have no notion of,
but by which good judges distinguish the master.
He attends even to their air, dress, and motions,
and imitates them liberally, and not servilely; he
copies, but does not mimic. These personal graces are of very great consequence. They antici-
pate the sentiments, before merit can engage the
understanding; they captivate the heart, and give
rise, I believe, to the extravagant notions of charms
and philtres. Their effects were so surprising, that
they were reckoned supernatural.

C

In short, as it is necessary to possess learning, honour, and virtue, to gain the esteem and admiration of mankind, so politeness and good breeding are equally necessary to render us agreeable in conversation and common life. Great talents are above the generality of the world, who neither possess them themselves, nor are competent judges of them in others: but all are judges of the lesser talents, such as civility, affability, and an agreeable address and manner; because they feel the good effects of them, as making society easy and agreeable.

To conclude: Be assured, that the profoundest learning, without good breeding, is unwelcome and tiresome pedantry; and good breeding, without learning, is but frivolous; whereas learning adds solidity to good breeding, and good breeding gives charms and graces to learning: that a man, who is not perfectly well-bred, is unfit for good company, and unwelcome in it; and that a man, who is not well-bred, is full as unfit for business as for company.

Make, then, good breeding the great object of your thoughts and actions. Observe carefully the behaviour and manners of those who are distinguished by their good breeding; imitate, nay, endeavour to excel, that you may at least reach them; and be convinced that good breeding is to all worldly qualifications, what charity is to all Christian virtues. Observe how it adorns merit, and how often it covers the want of it.

GRACES.*

THE graces of the person, the countenance, and

---

* We must not think it sufficient that we do any thing merely well: but we ought to make it our study to do every thing gracefully also.

the way of speaking, are essential things. The very same thing said by a genteel person in an engaging way, and gracefully and distinctly spoken, would please; which would shock, if muttered out by an awkward figure, with a sullen serious countenance. The poets represent Venus as attended

---

Now, grace is nothing more than a certain lustre, which shines forth from a harmony of the parts of things, properly connected and elegantly disposed in regard to the whole: without which symmetry, indeed, what is really good may not be beautiful; and without which, even beauty itself is not graceful, or even pleasing. And as a dish, however good or wholesome, is not likely to please our guests, if it has either no flavour at all, or a bad one; thus the behaviour of men, though it really offend no one, may, nevertheless, be insipid, and even distasteful, unless a man can learn that sweetness of manners, which, I apprehend, is properly called elegance and grace.

Wherefore, every kind of vice ought, indeed, on its own account, and without any other cause, to be esteemed extremely odious; for vice is a thing so very shocking, and unbecoming a gentleman, that every well-regulated and virtuous mind must feel pain and disgust at the ignominious appearance of it. He, therefore, that is desirous of appearing amiable in his conversation with mankind, ought, above all things, to shun every kind of vice; those especially which are the most shameful and base; such as luxury, avarice, cruelty, and the like: of which some are evidently vile and abject: such as gluttony and drunkenness: some filthy and obscene; such as lewdness; some shockingly wicked; as murder; and so of the rest. Every one of which is, in its own nature, some more, some less, peculiarly odious and detestable to others. Now all these vices in general, as things scandalous and unlawful, render a man thoroughly disagreeable in common life.—*Galateo.*

by the three Graces, to intimate, that even beauty
will not do without. Minerva ought to have three
also; for without them, learning has few attractions.

If we examine ourselves seriously, why particular people please and engage us, more than others
of equal merit, we shall always find that it is because the former have the Graces, and the latter
not. I have known many a woman, with an exact
shape, and a symmetrical assemblage of beautiful
features, please nobody; while others, with very
moderate shapes and features, have charmed every
body. It is certain that Venus will not charm so
much without her attendant Graces, as they will
without her. Among men, how often has the most
solid merit been neglected, unwelcome, or even re-
jected, for want of them! while flimsy parts, little
knowledge, and less merit, introduced by the Graces, have been received, cherished, and admired.

We proceed now to investigate what these Graces are, and to give some instructions for acquiring
them.

Address.

A man's fortune is frequently decided for ever by
his first address.* If it is pleasing, people are

---

* Every one should accustom himself to address others
in a kind and affable manner; converse with them, answer them, and behave to every one as he would to a fel-
low-citizen, and one with whom he was intimately acquainted. In this respect many people are greatly defective: who never vouchsafe to look pleased upon any
one; who seem glad of every opportunity to contradict
whatever other people assert; and, whatever act of kindness is tendered them, they reject it with rudeness; like

hurried involuntarily into a persuasion that he has
a merit, which possibly he has not: as, on the
other hand, if it is ungraceful, they are immediately prejudiced against him; and unwilling to allow
him the merit which, it may be, he has. The worst
bred man in Europe, should a lady drop her fan,
would certainly take it up and give it to her; the
best bred man in Europe could do no more. The
difference, however, would be considerable: the
latter would please by his graceful address in presenting it; the former would be laughed at for
doing it awkwardly. The carriage of a gentleman
should be genteel, and his motions graceful. He
should be particularly careful of his manner and
address, when he presents himself in company.
Let them be respectful without meanness, easy
without too much familiarity, genteel without affectation, and insinuating without any seeming art or
design. Men, as well as women, are much oftener
led by their hearts than by their understandings
The way to the heart is through the senses; please
their eyes and their ears, and the work is half done.

Art of Pleasing.

It is a very old and a very true maxim, that those
kings reign the most secure, and the most absolute,

---

foreigners or barbarians, who are suspicious of every civility that is shown them; who never discover the least
degree of cheerfulness, by any sprightly or even friendly
conversation; and whatever overture of respect is shown
them, they receive it with disdain. 'Mr. Such-a-one desired me to make his compliments to you.' 'What the
devil have I to do with his compliments?' 'Mr. —— in-
quired after you lately, and asked how you did.' 'Let
him come and feel my pulse, if he wants to know.' Now
men of this morose stamp are, deservedly, but little loved
or esteemed by others.—*Galateo.*

who reign in the hearts of their people. Their
popularity is a better guard than their army; and
the affections of their subjects, a better pledge of
their obedience, than their fears. This rule is, in
proportion, full as true, though upon a different
scale, with regard to private people. A man who
possesses that great art of pleasing universally, and
of gaining the affections of those with whom he
converses, possesses a strength which nothing else
can give him : a strength, which facilitates and
helps his rise; and which, in case of accidents,
breaks his fall. Few young people of your age
sufficiently consider this great point of popularity;
and when they grow older and wiser, strive in vain
to recover what they lost by their negligence.
There are three principal causes that hinder them
from acquiring this useful strength ; pride, inattention, and *mauvaise honte.* The first I will not,
cannot, suspect you of; it is too much below your
understanding. You cannot, and I am sure you
do not, think yourself superior by nature to the
Savoyard who cleans your room, or the footman
who cleans your shoes; but you may rejoice, and
with reason, at the difference which fortune has
made in your favour. Enjoy all those advantages;
but without insulting those who are unfortunate
enough to want them, or even doing any thing unnecessarily that may remind them of that want.
For my own part, I am more upon my guard as to
my behaviour to my servants, and others who are
called my inferiors, than I am towards my equals;
for fear of being suspected of that mean and ungenerous sentiment, of desiring to make others feel
that difference which fortune has, and perhaps, too,
undeservedly, made between us. Young people do

not enough attend to this; but falsely imagine that
the imperative mood, and a rough tone of authority and decision, are indications of spirit and
courage.

Inattention is always looked upon, though sometimes unjustly, as the effect of pride and contempt;
and where it is thought so, is never forgiven. In
this article, young people are generally exceedingly
to blame, and offend extremely. Their whole attention is engrossed by their particular set of acquaintance; and by some few glaring and exalted
objects of rank, beauty, or parts: all the rest they
think so little worth their care, that they neglect
even common civility towards them. I will frankly confess to you, that this was one of my great
faults when I was of your age. Very attentive to
please that narrow court-circle in which I stood en-
chanted, I considered every thing else as *bourgeois*,
and unworthy of common civility; I paid my court
assiduously and skilfully enough to shining and distinguished figures, such as ministers, wits, and
beauties; but then I most absurdly and imprudently neglected, and consequently offended, all others.
By this folly I made myself a thousand enemies of
both sexes; who, though I thought them very insignificant, found means to hurt me essentially,
where I wanted to recommend myself the most.
I was thought proud, though I was only imprudent. A general easy civility and attention
to the common run of ugly women, and of mid-
dling men, both which I sillily thought, called and
treated as odd people, would have made me as
many friends, as by the contrary conduct I made
myself enemies. All this too was *a pure perte*;
for I might equally, and even more successfully,

have made my court, where I had particular views
to gratify. I will allow that this task is often very
unpleasant, and that one pays, with some unwillingness, that tribute of attention to dull and tedious men, and to old and ugly women; but it is
the lowest price of popularity and general applause, which are very well worth purchasing,
were they much dearer. I conclude this head with
this advice to you: Gain, by particular assiduity
and address, the men and women you want; and,
by a universal civility and attention, please every
body so far as to have their good word, if not their
good will; or, at least, as to secure a partial neutrality.

Mauvaise honte not only hinders young people
from making a great many friends, but makes them
a great many enemies. They are ashamed of doing the thing that they know to be right, and would
otherwise do, for fear of the momentary laugh of
some fine gentleman or lady, or of some *mauvais
plaisant.* I have been in this case; and have often
wished an obscure acquaintance at the devil for
meeting and taking notice of me, when I was in
what I thought and called fine company. I have
returned their notice shily, awkwardly, and consequently offensively; for fear of a momentary joke;
not considering, as I ought to have done, that the
very people, who would have joked upon me at
first, would have esteemed me the more for it afterwards.

Pursue steadily, and without fear or shame,
whatever your reason tells you is right, and what
you see is practised by people of more experience
than yourself and of established characters of good
sense and good breeding.

After all this, perhaps you will say, that it is impossible to please every body. I grant it: but it does not follow that one should not therefore endeavour to please as many as one can. Nay, I will go farther, and admit, that it is impossible for any man not to have some enemies. But this truth, from long experience, I assert: that he who has the most friends, and the fewest enemies, is the strongest; will rise the highest with the least envy; and fall, if he does fall, the gentlest and the most pitied. This is surely an object worth pursuing. Pursue it according to the rules I have here given you. I will add one observation more, and two examples to enforce it; and then, as the parsons say, conclude.

The late Duke of Ormond was almost the weakest, but, at the same time, the best bred and most popular man in this kingdom. His education in courts and camps, joined to an easy, gentle nature, had given him that habitual affability, those engaging manners, and those mechanical attentions, that almost supplied the place of every talent he wanted; and he wanted almost every one. They procured him the love of all men, without the esteem of any. He was impeached after the death of Queen Anne, only because that, having been engaged in the same measures with those who were necessarily to be impeached, his impeachment for form's sake, became necessary. But he was impeached without acrimony, and without the least intention that he should suffer, notwithstanding the party-violence of those times. The question for his impeachment, in the House of commons, was carried by many fewer votes, than any other question of impeachment; and Earl Stanhope, then

Mr. Stanhope, and secretary of state, who impeached him, very soon after negociated and concluded his accommodation with the late king; to whom he was to have been presented the next day. But the late Bishop of Rochester, Atterbury, who thought that the Jacobite cause might suffer by losing the Duke of Ormond, went in all haste and prevailed with the poor weak man to run away; assuring him, that he was only to be gulled into a disgraceful submission, and not to be pardoned in consequence of it. When his subsequent attainder passed, it excited mobs and disturbances in town. He had not a personal enemy in the world, and had a thousand friends. All this was singly owing to his natural desire of pleasing; and to the mechanical means that his education, not his parts, had given him of doing it. The other instance is the late Duke of Marlborough, who studied the art of pleasing, because he well knew the importance of it: he enjoyed and used it more than ever man did. He gained whoever he had a mind to gain; and he had a mind to gain every body, because he knew that every body was more or less worth gaining. Though his power, as minister and general, made him many political and party enemies, they did not make him one personal one; and the very people who would gladly have displaced, disgraced, and perhaps attainted, the Duke of Marlborough, at the same time personally loved Mr. Churchill, even though his private character was blemished by sordid avarice, the most unamiable of all vices. He had wound up and turned his whole machine to please and engage. He had an inimitable sweetness and gentleness in his countenance, a a tenderness in his manner of speaking, a graceful dignity in every motion, and a universal and minute attention to the least things that could possibly please the least person. This was all art in him; art, of which he well knew and enjoyed the advantages: for no man ever had more interior ambition, pride, and avarice, than he had.

Choice of amusements.

A gentleman always attends even to the *choice* of his amusements. If at cards, he will not play at cribbage, all-fours, or putt; or, in sports of exercise, be seen at skittles, foot-ball, leap-frog, cricket, driving of coaches, &c. for he knows that such an imitation of the manners of the mob will indelibly stamp him with vulgarity. I cannot likewise avoid calling playing upon any musical instrument illiberal in a gentleman. Music is usually reckoned one of the liberal arts, and not unjustly; but a man of fashion, who is seen piping or fiddling at a concert, degrades his own dignity. If you love music, hear it; pay fiddlers to play to you, but never fiddle yourself. It makes a gentleman appear frivolous and contemptible, leads him frequently into bad company, and wastes that time which might otherwise be well employed.

Carving.

However trifling some things may seem, they are no longer so, when above half the world thinks them otherwise. Carving, as it occurs at least once in every day, is not below our notice. We should use ourselves to carve adroitly and genteelly, without hacking half an hour across a bone, without bespattering the company with the sauce, and without overturning the glasses into your neighbour's pockets. To be awkward in this particular, is extremely disagreeable and ridiculous. It is easily avoided by a little attention and use; and a man, who tells you gravely that he cannot carve, may as well tell you that he cannot blow his nose; it is both as easy and as necessary.*

---

* *Rules for behaviour at table.*

It is very rude, when at table, to scratch any part of your body.

You ought to take care, also, if possible, not to spit during that time; or, if you are under a necessity of doing it, it ought to be done in some decent manner. I have sometimes heard, that there were whole nations, formerly, so temperate, and of so dry a habit of body, from frequent exercise, that they never spit or blew their noses on any occasion. Why cannot we therefore contain our spittle for so short a space of time, at least, as is spent at our meals?

We should likewise be careful not to cram in our food so greedily, and with so voracious an appetite, as to cause us to hiccup, or be guilty of any thing else that may offend the eyes or the ears of the company; which they do who eat in such a hurry, as, by their puffing and blowing, to be troublesome to those who sit near them.

It is also very indecent to rub your teeth with the table-cloth or napkin; and to endeavour to pick them with your finger is more so.

In the presence also of others, to wash your mouth, and to squirt out the wine with which you have performed that operation, is very unpolite.

When the table is cleared, to carry about your toothpick in your mouth, like a bird going to build his nest, or to stick it behind your ear, as a barber does his comb, is no very genteel custom.

They also are undoubtedly mistaken in their notions of politeness, who carry their tooth-pick cases hanging down from their necks; for, besides that it is an odd sight

Chit-Chat.

Study to acquire that fashionable kind of *small-talk* or *chit-chat*, which prevails in all polite assemblies; and which, trifling as it may appear, is of

for a gentleman to produce any thing of that kind from his bosom, like some strolling pedlar, this inconvenience must also follow from such a practice, that he who acts thus discovers that he is but too well furnished with every instrument of luxury, and too anxious about every thing that relates to the belly: and I can see no reason why the same persons might not as well display a silver spoon hanging about their necks.

To lean with your elbows upon the table, or to fill both your cheeks so full that your jaws seem swelled, is by no means agreeable.

Neither ought you, by any token or gesture, to discover that you take too great pleasure in any kind of food or wine, which is a custom more proper for inn-keepers and parasites.

To invite those who sit at table with you to eat, by expressions of this kind, 'What! have you proclaimed a fast to-day?' or, 'Perhaps here is nothing at table you can make a dinner of?' or, 'Pray, sir, taste this or that dish:' Thus to invite people, I say, is by no means a laudable custom, though now become familiar to almost every one, and practised in every family; for though these officious people show that the person whom they thus invite is really the object of their care, yet they give occasion, by this means, to the person invited, to be less free in his behaviour, and make him blush at the thought of being the subject of observation.

For any one to take upon him to help another to any thing that is set upon the table, I do not think very polite; unless, perhaps, the person who does this is of much superior dignity, so that he who receives it is honoured by the offer; for if this be done amongst equals, he that offers any thing to another, appears, in some mea-

use in mixed companies and at table.   It turns
upon the public events of Europe, and then is at its
best; very often upon the number, the goodness
or badness, the discipline or the clothing, of the
troops of different princes; sometimes upon the families, the marriages, the relations of princes and
considerable people; and sometimes the magnifi-
cence of public entertainments, balls, masquerades,
&c.   Upon such occasions, likewise, it is not amiss
to know how to *parler cuisine*, and to be able to
dissert upon the growth and flavour of wines.
These, it is true, are very little things; but they
are little things that occur very often, and therefore should be said *avec gentillesse et grace.*

Cleanliness.

The person should be accurately clean; the teeth,
hands, and nails, should be particularly so; a dirty mouth has real ill consequences to the owner;

---

sure, to affect a superiority over him: sometimes, too,
what is offered may not be agreeable to the palate of
another. Besides, a man by this means seems to intimate
that the entertainment is not very liberally furnished out;
or, at least, that the dishes are placed in a preposterous
order, when one abounds and the other wants. And it is
possible that the person who gives the entertainment may
not be very well pleased with such a freedom. Nevertheless, in this respect, we ought rather to do what is usually
done, than what we may think would be better done: for
it is more advisable, in cases of this nature, to err with
the multitude, than to be singular even in acting rightly.
But whatever may be proper or improper in this respect,
you should never refuse any thing that is offered you; for
you will be thought either to despise or to reprove him
that offers it.—*Galateo.*

for it infallibly causes the decay, as well as the intolerable pain, of the teeth; and is very offensive, for it will most inevitably stink. Nothing looks more ordinary, vulgar, and illiberal, than dirty hands, and ugly, uneven, and ragged nails; the ends of which should be kept smooth and clean, (not tipped with black,) and small segments of circles; and every time that the hands are wiped, rub the skin round the nails backwards, that it may not grow up, and shorten them too much. Upon no account whatever put your fingers in your nose or ears. It is the most shocking, nasty, vulgar rudeness, that can be offered to company. The ears should be washed well every morning; and, in blowing your nose, never look at it afterwards.*

These things may, perhaps, appear too insignificant to be mentioned; but when it is remembered that a thousand little nameless things, which every one feels but no one can describe, conspire to form that *whole* of pleasing, I think we ought not to call them trifling. Besides, a clean shirt and a clean person are as necessary to health as not to offend other people. I have ever held it as a maxim, and which I have lived to see verified, that a man who

* It is extremely indecent to spit, cough, and expectorate, (as it were,) in company, as some hearty fellows are apt to do; and more so, when you have blown your nose, to draw aside and examine the contents of your handkerchief: as if you expected pearls or rubies to distil from your brain. These kinds of habits, in good company, are so very nauseous and disgusting, that, if we indulge ourselves in them, no one can be very fond of our acquaintance. So far from it, that even those who are inclined to wish us well, must, by these and the like disagreeable customs, be entirely alienated from us.— *Galateo.*

is negligent at twenty, will be a sloven at forty, and
intolerable at fifty years of age.

Compliments.*

Attend to the compliments of congratulation, or
condolence, that you hear a well-bred man make
to his superiors, to his equals, and to his inferiors;
watch even his countenance and his tone of voice;
for they all conspire in the main point of pleasing.
There is a certain distinguishing diction of a man
of fashion: he will not content himself with saying,
like John Trott, to a new married man, 'Sir, I wish
you much joy:' or to a man who has lost his son,
'Sir, I am sorry for your loss;' and both with a
countenance equally unmoved: but he will say in
effect the same thing, in a more elegant and less
trivial manner, and with a countenance adapted to
the occasion. He will advance with warmth, vivacity, and a cheerful countenance to the new-mar-
ried man, and, embracing him, perhaps, say to him,
'If you do justice to my attachment to you, you

---

* If in your country it be a customary thing to say to
any one, when you take your leave of him, 'Sir, I kiss
your hand with the most profound respect:' or, 'Sir I am
your most obedient servant, and entirely at your devotion:' or, 'Sir, you may command my best services; use
me or abuse me, at your pleasure, and on every occasion
whatever.' If, I say, it be the fashion to use these and
the like forms of expression, I would by all means have
you make use of them as well as other people.

In short, whether in taking leave of, or in writing to,
any person, you ought to address him, or take leave of
him, not as reason, but as custom, requires; not as men
used to do formerly, or as, perhaps, they ought to do;
but as they do now at this present time.— *Galateo.*

will judge of the joy that I feel upon this occasion, better than I can express it, &c.' To the other in affliction he will advance slowly, with a grave composure of countenance, in a more deliberate manner, and with a lower voice, perhaps, say, 'I hope you will do me the justice to be convinced, that I feel whatever you feel, and shall ever be affected where you are concerned.'

Diction.

There is a certain language of conversation, a fashionable diction, of which every gentleman ought to be perfectly master, in whatever language he speaks. The French attend to it carefully, and with great reason; and their language, which is a language of phrases, helps them out exceedingly. That delicacy of diction is characteristical of a man of fashion and good company.*

---

* In any continued speech or narration, your words ought to be so placed, as the ease of common conversation requires; I mean, that they should neither be perplexed and intricate, nor too ambitiously transposed, which many are apt to do, from a certain affectation of elegance; whose discourse is more like the forms of a notary, who is explaining some instrument to others, in their vernacular tongue, which he has written in Latin, than to the speech of one man talking to another in the language of their own country. A style thus transposed and perplexed may sometimes answer the end of a man that is making verses, but is always ungraceful in a familiar conversation.

Nor ought we only to abstain from this poetical manner of speaking in common conversation, but also from the pompous method of those that speak in public; for unless we observe this caution, our discourse will be disagreeable and extremely disgusting; though, perhaps, it

Dress and dancing.

Dress is one of the various ingredients that contribute to the art of pleasing, and, therefore, an ob-

is a matter of greater skill to make those solemn speeches, than to converse with a man in private; but then, that kind of eloquence must be reserved for its proper place. A man ought not to dance, but walk a common pace along the street; for though all men can walk, whereas many people cannot dance, yet the latter ought to be reserved for a wedding, or some joyful occasion, and not to be practised in the public walks. This way of conversing, then, so full of ostentation, ought by all means to be avoided.

Nor yet would I have you, for this reason, accustom yourself to a mean and abject manner of expressing yourself; such as the lowest dregs of the people, porters, cobblers, and laundresses, use; but rather, that you should imitate the conversation of a well-bred man and a person of fashion. How to accomplish this, I shall now point out to you; namely,

First, By never discoursing upon low, frivolous, dirty, or immoderate subjects.

Secondly, By making choice of such words in your own language, as are clear, proper, well-sounding, and such as have usually a good meaning annexed to them, and do not suggest to the imagination the idea of any thing base, filthy, or indecent.

Thirdly, By ranging your words in an elegant order, so that they may not appear confused, and jumbled together at random, nor, yet, by too laboured an exactness, forced into certain regular feet and measures.

Farther, By taking care to pronounce carefully and distinctly what you have to say; and not join together things entirely different and dissimilar.

If, moreover, in your discourse you are not too slow, like a man who, at a plentiful table, does not know what to choose first; nor yet too eager, like a man half-starv-

ject of some attention; for we cannot help forming
some opinion of a man's sense and character from
his dress. All affectation in dress implies a flaw
in the understanding. Men of sense carefully
avoid any particular character in their dress; they
are actually clean for their own sake, but all the
rest is for the sake of other people. A man should
dress as well, and in the same manner, as the people of sense and fashion of the place where he is:
if he dresses more than they, he is a fop; if he
dresses less, he is unpardonably negligent: but of
the two, a young fellow should be rather too much
than too little dressed; the excess of that side will
wear off with a little age and reflection.

The difference in dress between a man and a
fop is, that the fop values himself upon his dress;
and the man of sense laughs at it, at the same time
that he knows that he must not neglect it. There
are a thousand foolish customs of this kind, which,
as they are not criminal, must be complied with,
and even cheerfully, by men of sense. Diogenes,
the Cynic, was a wise man for despising them, but
a fool for showing it.

---

ed; but, if you speak calmly and deliberately as a moderate man ought to do.

Lastly, if you pronounce each letter and syllable with
a proper sweetness (yet, not like some pedagogue, who
is teaching children to read and spell,) neither stifling
your word between your teeth, as if you were chewing
them; or huddling them together, as if you were swal-
lowing them. By carefully attending to these precepts
then; and a few more of this kind, others will hear you
gladly and with pleasure; and you yourself will obtain,
with applause, that degree of dignity which becomes a
well-bred man and a gentleman.—*Galateo.*

We should not attempt to rival or excel a fop in dress; but it is necessary to dress, to avoid singularity and ridicule. Great care should be taken to be always dressed like the reasonable people of our own age, in the place where we are, whose dress is never spoken of, one way or another, as neither too negligent nor too much studied.*

Awkwardness of carriage is very alienating, and a total negligence of dress and air an impertinent insult upon custom and fashion. Women have

---

* Let your dress be conformable to the customs of the age you live in, and suitable to your condition; for it is not in our power to alter the general fashions at our pleasure; which, as they are produced, so they are swallowed up, by time. In the mean while, every one may make shift to accommodate the general fashion to his own particular convenience, as the case may require. Thus, (for instance,) if you happen to have longer legs than the rest of mankind, and short coats are in vogue, you may take care that your coat be not the very shortest; but rather somewhat less short than the extremity of the fashion requires: or if any one has either too slender, or too fleshy, or even distorted legs, let not such a one distinguish himself by stockings of a scarlet or any other very conspicuous colour, that he may not attract the notice of others to his defects.

No part of your dress ought to be either too splendid, or enormously fringed or laced, lest, perhaps, you should be said to have stolen Cupid's mantle or the buskins of Ganymede.

But whatever your clothes are, take care that they be well made; that they will sit with a grace, and be fitted to your person; that you may not appear to have borrowed them of a friend, or hired them for the day: but, above all things, they should be suited to your rank and profession; that a scholar be not dressed like a soldier, or an officer like a buffoon or dancing-master.—*Galateo.*

great influence as to a man's fashionable character;
and an awkward man will never have their votes,
which are very numerous, and oftener counted
than weighed.

When we are once well dressed for the day, we
should think no more of it afterwards; and, without any stiffness for fear of discomposing that
dress, we should be as easy and natural as if we
had no clothes on at all.

Dancing, likewise, though a silly trifling thing, is
one of those established follies which people of
sense are sometimes obliged to conform to; and, if
they do, they should be able to perform it well.

In dancing, the motion of the arms should be
particularly attended to, as these decide a man's
being genteel or otherwise, more than any other
part of the body. A twist or stiffness in the wrist
will make any man look awkward. If a man dances well from the waist upwards, wears his hat well,
and moves his head properly, he dances well.
Coming into a room and presenting yourself to a
company should be also attended to, as this always
gives the first impression, which is often indelible.
Those who present themselves well, have a certain
dignity in their air, which, without the least seeming mixture of pride, at once engages and is respected.

Drinking of healths.

Drinking of healths is now growing out of fashion, and is deemed unpolite in good company.
Custom once had rendered it universal, but the
improved manners of the age now consider it as absurd and vulgar. What can be more rude or ridiculous than to interrupt persons at their meals with

an unnecessary compliment? Abstain, then, from this silly custom where you find it disused; and use it only at those tables where it continues general. *

Assurance.

A steady assurance is too often improperly styled impudence. For my part, I see no impudence, but, on the contrary, infinite utility and advantage, in presenting one's self with the same coolness and

---

* To drink to any one, and tease him to pledge you in larger glasses, against his inclination, is, in itself, an execrable custom; which, however, has so far prevailed, as to appear impossible almost ever to be abolished. But you will, I am persuaded, gladly abstain from this vile practice; though, if you should be urged by others, and cannot entirely resist their importunity, you may thank them, and say that you willingly yield them the victory; or, without taking a larger draught, you may lightly taste what is presented to you.

And indeed this custom of drinking healths is sufficiently ancient; and was formerly much practised in Greece itself; for Socrates is highly applauded by some writers, that, after spending the whole night in drinking largely with Aristophanes, as soon as it was light in the morning, he would delineate and demonstrate any the most subtle geometrical problem without the least hesitation; an evident proof, indeed, that the wine had not yet done him any injury: but this is rather to be ascribed to the strength of his brain, and to a good constitution, than to the temperance of a philosopher. Yet from this instance, and other frivolous arguments, some people have endeavoured to prove the expediency of drinking freely sometimes; though I can by no means assent to their opinion; notwithstanding that, by a pompous parade of words, some learned men have so managed it, that an unjust cause has often gained the victory, and reason submitted to sophistry and chicane.—*Galateo.*

unconcern in any and every company : till one can
do that, I am very sure that one can never present
one's self well. Whatever is done under concern
and embarrassment, must be ill done ; and till a
man is absolutely easy and unconcerned in every
company, he will never be thought to have kept
good, nor be very welcome in it. Assurance and
intrepidity, under the white banner of seeming modesty clear the way to merit, that would otherwise
be discouraged by difficulties in its journey: whereas bare-faced impudence is the noisy and blustering
harbinger of a worthless and senseless usurper.

Hurry.

A man of sense may be in haste, but can never
be in a hurry, because he knows, that whatever he
does in a hurry he must necessarily do very ill.
He may be in haste to dispatch an affair, but he
will take care not to let that haste hinder his doing
it well. Little minds are in a hurry, when the object proves (as it commonly does) too big for them;
they run, they hare, they puzzle, confound, and
perplex themselves; they want to do every thing at
once, and never do it at all. But a man of sense
takes the time necessary for doing the thing he is
about well; and his haste to dispatch a business
only appears by the continuity of his application
to it: he pursues it with a cool steadiness, and fi-
nishes it before he begins any other.

Laughter.

Frequent and loud laughter is the characteristic
of folly and ill-manners :* it is the manner in

---

* We ought also to abstain from a foolish, rustic, and
insipid, horse-laugh, merely because we have contracted

which the mob expresses their silly joy at silly things; and they call it being merry. In my mind, there is nothing so illiberal, and so ill-bred, as audible laughter. True wit or sense never yet made any body laugh; they are above it; they please the mind, and give a cheerfulness to the countenance. But it is low buffoonery, or silly accidents, that always excite laughter; and that is what people of sense and breeding should show themselves above. A man's going to sit down, in the supposition that he has a chair behind him, and falling down upon his breech for want of one, sets a whole company laughing, when all the wit in the world would not do it; a plain proof, in my mind, how low and unbecoming a thing laughter is; not to mention the disagreeable noise that it makes, and the shocking distortion of the face that it occasions.

Many people, at first, from awkwardness, have got a very disagreeable and silly trick of laughing whenever they speak: and I know men of very good parts, who cannot say the commonest thing without laughing; which makes those who do not know them, take them at first for natural fools.

Letter-writing.

It is of the utmost importance to write letters well; as this is a talent which daily occurs, as well in business as in pleasure; and inaccuracies in orthography, or in style, are never pardoned but in

a silly habit of laughing, perhaps, rather from any necessity there is for it: nor ought you to laugh at any joke or smart saying of your own; for you will be thought to applaud your own wit. It belongs to the company, and not to him who says a good thing, to express their approbation by a laugh.— *Galateo.*

ladies: nor is it hardly pardonable in them. The
Epistles of Cicero are the most perfect models of
good writing.

Letters should be easy and natural, and convey
to the persons to whom we send them, just what we
would say to those persons if we were present with
them.

The best models of letter-writing are Cicero,
Cardinal d'Ossat, Madame Sevigne, and Comte
Bussy Rabutin. Cicero's Epistles to Atticus, and
to his familiar friends, are the best examples in the
friendly and the familiar style. The simplicity and
clearness of the Letters of Cardinal d'Oss .t show
how letters of business ought to be written. For
gay and amusing letters, there are none that equal
Comte Bussy's and Madame Sevigne's. They are
so natural, that they seem to be the extempore conversations of two people of wit, rather than letters.

Neatness in folding up, sealing, and directing
letters, is by no means to be neglected. There is
something in the exterior, even of a letter, that
may please or displease, and consequently deserves
some attention.

Nickname.

There is nothing that a young man, at his first
appearance in the world, has more reason to dread,
and therefore should take more pains to avoid, than
having any ridicule fixed on him. In the opinion
even of the most rational men it will degrade him,
but ruin him with the rest. Many a man has been
undone by acquiring a ridiculous nickname. The
causes of nicknames among well-bred men, are
generally the little defects in manner, elocution,
air, or address. To have the appellation of mut-
tering, awkward, ill-bred, absent, left-legged, an-

nexed always to your name, would injure you more than you imagine: avoid, then, these little defects, and you may set ridicule at defiance.

Pronunciation in speaking.

To acquire a graceful utterance, read aloud to some friend every day, and beg of him to interrupt and correct you whenever you read too fast, do not observe the proper stops, lay a wrong emphasis, or utter your words unintelligibly. You may even read aloud to yourself, and tune your utterance to your own ear. Take care to open your teeth when you read or speak, and articulate every word distinctly; which last cannot be done but by sounding the final letter. But, above all, study to vary your voice according to the subject, and avoid a monotony. Daily attention to these articles will, in a little time, render them easy and habitual to you.

The voice and manner of speaking, too, are not to be neglected: some people almost shut their mouths when they speak, and mutter so, that they are not to be understood; others speak so fast, and sputter, that they are not to be understood neither. some always speak as loud as if they were talking to deaf people; and others so low that one cannot hear them. All these habits are awkward and disagreeable, and are to be avoided by attention: they are the distinguishing marks of the ordinary people, who have had no care taken of their education. You cannot imagine how necessary it is to mind all these little things; for I have seen many people, with great talents, ill received for want of having these talents; and others well received, only from their little talents, and who had no great ones.

Spelling.

Orthography, or spelling well, is so absolutely
necessary for a man of letters or a gentleman, that
one false spelling may fix a ridicule on him for the
remainder of his life.   Reading carefully will contribute in a great measure to preserve you from exposing yourself by false spelling; for books are
generally well spelled, according to the orthography of the times.   Sometimes words, indeed, are
spelled differently by different authors, but those
instances are rare; and where there is only one
way of spelling a word, should you spell it wrong,
you will be sure to be ridiculed.   Nay, a *woman* of
a tolerable education would despise and laugh at
her lover if he should send her an ill spelled *billet-
doux.*

Style.

Style is the dress of thoughts; and let them be
ever so just, if your style is homely, coarse, and
vulgar, they will appear to as much disadvantage,
and be as ill received, as your person, though ever
so well proportioned, would, if dressed in rags,
dirt, and tatters.   It is not every understanding that
can judge of matter: but every ear can and does
judge, more or less of style. *

---

* We ought to make use of clear and significant
words; which we shall do, if we know how to make a
prudent choice of such words as are originally of our
own country: so that they are not too stale and obsolete,
and, like torn or thread-bare garments, laid aside and
out of use.   Such, in English, are *welkin, guerdon lore,
mead, eftsoons,* and the like.   The better to accomplish
this also, let your words be simple, and not ambiguous;
for it is in the construction of riddles that words are to

Mind your diction, in whatever language you
either write or speak: contract a habit of correctness and elegance. Consider your style, even in
the freest conversation and most familiar letters.
After, at least, if not before, you have said a thing,
reflect if you could not have said it better.

Writing.

Every man who has the use of his eyes and his
right hand can write whatever hand he pleases.
Nothing is so ungentleman-like as a school-boy's

---

be taken equivocally, or as expressing two different
things For the same reason, we ought to use words in
the most proper sense, and such as express the thing intended as significantly as possible, and which are the least
applicable to any other thing ; for by this means the very
objects themselves will seem to be represented to our
eyes, and rather pointed out to us, than merely described.
Thus, it is proper 'to a horse to *neigh*, to a dog to *bark*,
to a hog to *grunt*, to a bull to *bellow*, to a sheep to *bleat*,
to a boar to *gnash*, and to a serpent to *hiss*.'* As, therefore, the genuine and proper names of things are to be
used in our conversation with others, no one can commo-
diously converse with him who does not understand the
language which he makes use of: yet, though a stranger
may not be master of the language which we use, we are
not on his account to corrupt or lay aside our native
tongue; as some coxcomical jackanapes will attempt,
with violent efforts, to make use of the language of any
foreigner with whom they converse, and so express every
thing improperly. We ought never to make use of a
foreign language, unless when it is absolutely necessary
to express our wants: but in our common intercourse with
others, let us be contented with our native tongue, though
it may be thought far inferior to, and less noble than,
some others.—*Galateo.*

  * This precision in our language is of consequence;
and too much neglected.

scrawl. I do not desire you to write a stiff, formal hand, like that of a schoolmaster, but a genteel, legible, and liberal character, and to be able to write quick. As to the correctness and elegancy of your writing, attention to grammar does the one and to the best authors, the other. Epistolary correspondence should be easy and natural, and convey to the persons just what we would say if we were with them.

Vulgar expressions.

Vulgarism in language is a certain characteristic of bad company and a bad education. Proverbial expressions and trite sayings are the flowers of the rhetoric of a vulgar man. Would he say, that men differ in their tastes; he both supports and adorns that opinion by the good old saying, as he respectfully calls it, that 'What is one man's meat is another man's poison.' If any body attempts being *smart*, as he calls it, upon him, he gives them *tit for tat*, aye, that he does. He has always some favourite word for the time being, which, for the sake of using often, he commonly abuses; such as *vastly* angry, *vastly* kind, *vastly* handsome, and *vastly* ugly. Even his pronunciation of proper words carries the mark of the beast along with it. He calls the earth *yearth;* he is *obleged*, not *obliged*, to you. He goes *to wards*, and not *towards*, such a place. He sometimes affects hard words, by way of ornament, which he always mangles like a learned woman. A man of fashion never has recourse to proverbs and vulgar aphorisms; uses neither favourite words nor hard words; but takes great care to speak very correctly and grammatically, and to pronounce properly;

that is, according to the usage of the best companies. *

---

* Every gentleman will also be very cautious not to use
any indecent or immodest expressions. Now the decency of an expression consists either in the sound, or in the
word itself, or else in the signification of it; for there are
some words expressive of things decent enough, and yet
in the word itself, or in the sound of it, there seems to be
something indecent and unpolite. When, therefore,
words of this kind, though but slightly suspected, offer
themselves, well-bred women usually substitute others
more decent in their rooom: but you will meet with some
ladies (not the most polite women in the world) who frequently and inconsiderately let fall some expression or
other, which, if it were designedly named before them,
they would blush up to the ears. Women, therefore, who
either are, or wish to be, thought well-bred, should carefully guard, not only against all actions, but all words,
which are indecent or immodest; and not only so, but
from all which may appear such, or be capable of such an
interpretation.

It may farther be observed, that where two or more
words express the same thing, yet one may be more or
less decent than the other: for instance, we may decent-
ly enough say, 'He spent the night with the lady:' but if
we should express the same thing by another and more
plain phrase, it would be very improper to be mentioned.
Thus it becomes a lady, and even a well-bred man, to
describe a common prostitute by the name of an immodest woman, and so of the rest.

Nor are indecent and immodest words alone, but also
low and mean expressions, to be avoided, especially upon
great and illustrious subjects; for which reason, a poet,
otherwise of no vulgar merit, is deservedly reprehensi-
ble, who, intending to describe the splendour of a clear
sky, says,

'——— and without dregs the day :'

for so low and dirty a phrase was, in my opinion, by no.

Cautions against sundry odd habits.

Humming a tune within ourselves, drumming with our fingers, making a noise with our feet, and such awkward habits, being all breaches of good manners; are therefore indications of our contempt for the persons present, and consequently should not be practised.

Eating very quick, or very slow, is characteristic of vulgarity: the former infers poverty; the latter, if abroad, that you are disgusted with your entertainment and, if at home, that you are rude enough to give your friends what you cannot eat yourself. Eating soup with your nose in your plate is also vulgar: so likewise is smelling to the meat while on the fork, before you put it in your mouth. If you dislike what is sent upon your plate, leave it: but never by smelling to or examining it, appear to tax your friend with placing unwholesome provisions before you.

Spitting on the floor or carpet is a filthy practice, and which, were it to become general, would render it as necessary to change the carpets as the table-cloths. Not to add, it will induce our acquaintance to suppose that we have not been used to genteel furniture: for which reason alone, if for no other, a man of liberal education should avoid it.

---

means suitable to so splendid and illustrious an object: neither can any one cleverly call the sun 'the candle of the world;' for this expression suggests to the imagination of the reader the stink of tallow and the greasiness of the kitchen. Hither may be referred many of those proverbs which are in the mouth of every one: the sentiments of which may be good, but the words are polluted, as it were, by the familiar use of the vulgar, as every one may observe from daily experience.— *Galatea.*

To conclude this article. Never walk fast in the streets, which is a mark of vulgarity, ill befitting the character of a gentleman or a man of fashion, though it may be tolerable in a tradesman.

To stare any person full in the face, whom you may chance to meet, is an act also of ill breeding; it would seem to bespeak as if you saw something wonderful in his appearance, and is therefore a tacit reprehension.

Keep yourself free, likewise, from all odd tricks or habits; such as scratching yourself, putting your fingers to your mouth, nose, and ears, thrusting out your tongue, snapping your fingers, biting your nails, rubbing your hands, sighing aloud, and affected shivering of your body, gaping, and many others which I have noticed before: all which are imitations of the manners of the mob, and degrading to a gentleman.

KNOWLEDGE OF THE WORLD.

We should endeavour to hoard up, while we are young, a great stock of knowledge; for, though during that time of dissipation we may not have occasion to spend much of it, yet a time will come when we shall want it to maintain us.

How to acquire a knowledge of the world.

The knowledge of the world is only to be acquired in the world, and not in a closet. Books alone will never teach it you; but they will suggest many things to your observation, which might otherwise escape you; and your own observations upon mankind, when compared with those which you will find in books, will help you to fix the true point.

To know mankind well, requires full as much

attention and application as to know books, and,
it may be, more sagacity and discernment. I am,
at this time, acquainted with many elderly people,
who have all passed their whole lives in the great
world, but with such levity and inattention, that
they know no more of it, now than they did at fif-
teen. Do not flatter yourself, therefore, with the
thoughts that you can acquire this knowledge in the
frivolous-chit-chat of idle companies : no, you must
go much deeper than that. You must look into people, as well as at them: search, therefore, with the
greatest care into the characters of all those whom
you converse with; endeavour to discover their
predominant passions, their prevailing weaknesses,
their vanities, their follies, and their humours;
with all the right and wrong, wise and silly, springs
of human actions, which make such inconsistent
and whimsical beings of us, rational creatures.

Never show a contempt for any one.

There are no persons so insignificant and inconsiderable, but may, some time or other, or in something or other, have it in their power to be of use
to you; which they certainly will not, if you have
once shewn them contempt. Wrongs are often forgiven, but contempt never is: our pride remembers
it for ever. Remember, therefore, most carefully
to conceal your contempt, however just, wherever
you would not make an implacable enemy. Men
are much more unwilling to have their weaknesses
and their imperfections known, than their crimes;
and if you hint to a man that you think him silly,
ignorant, or even ill-bred or awkward, he will hate
you more and longer, than if you tell him plainly
that you think him a rogue. D 2

Make no man feel his inferiority.

Nothing is more insulting than to take pains to make a man feel a mortifying inferiority in knowledge, rank, fortune, &c. In the first, it is both ill-bred and ill-natured; and in the two latter articles, it is unjust, they not being in his power. Good breeding and good-nature incline us rather to raise people up to ourselves, than to mortify and depress them; besides it is making ourselves so many friends, instead of so many enemies.[*] A constant attention to please is a most necessary ingredient in the art of pleasing: it flatters the self-love of those to whom it is shown: it engages and captivates, more than things of much greater importance. Every man is in some measure obliged to discharge the social duties of life: but these attentions are voluntary acts, the free-will offerings of good-breeding, and good-nature: they are received, remembered, and returned, as such. Women, in particular, have a righ to them; and any omission in that respect is down right ill-breeding.

Never expose people's weaknesses and infirmities.

We should never yield to that temptation, which to most young men is very strong, of exposing other people's weaknesses and infirmities, for the sake either of diverting the company, or of showing our own superiority. We may, by that means, get the laugh on our side for the present, but we shall make

---

[*] Nothing ought to be done in the presence of those whom we are desirous to please, which may exhibit an appearance of superiority rather than an equality of condition. But every action and every gesture should be such as may testify the greatest respect and esteem for the persons with whom we are in company.—*Cul iter.*

enemies by it for ever; and even those who laugh
with us will, upon reflection, fear and despise us:
it is ill-natured; and a good heart desires rather to
conceal than expose other people's weaknesses or
misfortunes. If we have wit, we should use it to
please, and not to hurt: we may shine, like the sun
in the temperate zones, without scorching.*

---

* We ought not to ridicule or to make sport even of our
greatest enemy; it being a mark of greater contempt to
laugh at a person, than to do him any real injury: for all
injuries are done either through resentment or some covetous disposition; but there is no one who conceives any
resentment against any person, or on account of any
thing, which he does not at all value, or who covets that
which is universally despised; which shows, that they
think him a man of some consequence, at least, whom
they injure; but that they have an utter contempt for him
whom they ridicule, or make a jest of: for when we
make sport of any one, in order to expose or put him out
of countenance, we do not act thus with a view to any advantage or emolument, but for our pleasure and diversion.
We ought, by all means, therefore, in our common intercourse with mankind, to abstain from this ignominious
kind of ridicule. And this is not very carefully attended
to by those who remind others of their foibles, either by
their words or their gestures, or by rudely mentioning
the thing itself; as many do, who slily mimic, either by
their speech or by some ridiculous distortion of their person, those that stammer, or who are bandy-legged, or
hump-backed; or, in short, who ridicule others for being
any ways deformed, distorted, or of a dwarfish and insignificant appearance; or those who, with laughing and
exultation, triumph over others for expressing themselves
with any little impropriety, or who take a pleasure in
putting them to the blush; which practices, as they are
very disagreeable, so they make us deservedly odious.
Not much unlike these are those buffoons, who take a

Steady command of temper and countenance.

There are many inoffensive arts which are necessary in the course of the world, and which he

pleasure in teazing and ridiculing any one that comes in
their way; not so much out of contempt, or with an intention to affront them, as merely for their own diversion. And, certainly, there would be no difference between jesting upon a person and making a jest of him,
but that the end and intention are different: for he that
jests upon any one, does it merely for amusement; but he
who makes a jest of him, does it out of contempt. Although these two expressions are usually confounded,
both in writing and in conversation, yet he that makes a
joke of another, sets him in an ignominious light for his
own pleasure; whereas he who only jokes upon him,
cannot so properly be said to take pleasure, as to divert
himself in seeing another involved in some harmless error; for he himself, probably, would be very much grie-
ved and concerned to see the same person in any ludicrous
circumstances, attended with real disgrace.

Hence it appears, that one and the same thing, though
done to one and the same person, may be sometimes taken
as jesting upon a man, and sometimes as making a jest
of him, according to the intention of the person that does
it. But because our intention cannot be evidently known
to other people, it is not a very prudent practice, in our
daily commerce with the world, to make use of so ambi
guous and suspected an art.

Not to mention, at present, that many of these wagge-
ries consist, in some sort, of *deception*. Now, every one
is naturally provoked at being *deceived* or led into an
error. It appears, then, from many considerations, that
he who is desirous of gaining the love and good-will of
mankind, ought not greatly to affect this superiority in
playing upon and teazing those with whom he converses.

It is true, indeed, that we cannot, by any means, pass
through this calamitous mortal life without some recrea-

who practises the earliest will please the most and rise the soonest. The spirits and vivacity of youth are apt to neglect them as useless, or reject them as troublesome: but subsequent knowledge and experience of the world remind us of their importance, commonly when it is too late. The principle of these things is the mastery of one's temper, and that coolness of mind and serenity of countenance which hinder us from discovering, by words, actions, or even looks, those passions or sentiments by which we are inwardly moved or agitated; and the discovery of which gives cooler and abler people such infinite advantages over us, not only in great business, but in all the most common occurrences of life. A man who does not possess himself enough to hear disagreeable things without visible marks of anger and change of countenance,

---

tion and amusement; and because wit and humour occasion mirth and laughter, and consequently that relaxation which the mind requires, we are generally fond of those who excel in a facetious and agreeable kind of raillery, and, therefore, the contrary to what I have asserted may seem to be true; I mean, that in our ordinary intercourse with mankind, it is highly commendable to entertain each other with wit and facetious repartees; and, doubtless, those who have the art of rallying with a good grace, and in an agreeable manner, are much more amiable than people of a contrary character.

But here regard must be had to many circumstances; and since the end proposed by these jocose people is to create mirth, by leading some one, whom they really esteem into some harmless error, it is requisite that the error into which he is led be of such a kind, as not to be attended with any considerable detriment or disgrace; otherwise, this sort of jokes can hardly be distinguished from real injuries.—*Galateo.*

or agreeable ones without sudden bursts of joy and expansion of countenance, is at the mercy of every artful knave or pert coxcomb : the former will provoke or please you by design, to catch unguarded words or looks; by which he will easily decipher the secrets of your heart, of which you should keep the key yourself, and trust it with no man living. The latter will, by his absurdity, and without intending it, produce the same discoveries, of which other people will avail themselves.

If you find yourself subject to sudden starts of passion, or madness, (for I see no difference between them, but in their duration,) resolve within yourself, at least, never to speak one word while you feel that emotion within you.

In short, make yourself absolute master of your temper and your countenance; so far, at least, as that no visible change do appear in either, whatever you may feel inwardly. This may be difficult, but it is by no means impossible; and as a man of sense never attempts impossibilities on the one hand, on the other, he is never discouraged by difficulties : on the contrary, he redoubles his industry and his diligence; he perseveres, and infallibly prevails at last. In any point which prudence bids you pursue, and which a manifest utility attends, let difficulties only animate your industry, not deter you from the pursuit. If one way has failed, try another: be active, persevere, and you will conquer. Some people are to be reasoned, some flattered, some intimidated, and some teazed, into a thing; but, in general, all are to be brought into it at last, if skilfully applied to, properly managed, and indefatigably attacked in their several weak places. The time should likewise be judiciously chosen: every man has his *mollia tempora*, but that is far from being all day long; and you would choose your time very ill, if you applied to a man about one business, when his head was full of another, or when his heart was full of grief, anger, or any other disagreeable sentiment.

Judge of other men's by your own feelings.

In order to judge of the inside of others, study your own; for men, in general, are very much alike; and though one has one prevailing passion, and another has another, yet their operations are much the same; and whatever engages or disgusts, pleases or offends you, in others, will *mutatis mutandis*, engage, disgust, please, or offend others, in you. Observe, with the utmost attention, all the operations of your own mind, the nature of your passions, and the various motives that determine your will; and you may, in a great degree, know all mankind. For instance: Do you find yourself hurt and mortified, when another makes you feel his superiority and your own inferiority, in knowledge, parts, rank, or fortune? you will certainly take great care not to make a person, whose good will, good word, interest, esteem, or friendship, you would gain, feel that superiority in you, in case you have it. If disagreeable insinuations, sly sneers, or repeated contradictions, tease and irritate you, would you use them where you wished to engage and please? Surely not: and I hope you wish to engage and please almost universally. The temptation of saying a smart and witty thing, or *bon mot*, and the malicious applause with which it is commonly received, have made people who can say them, and still oftener people who think they can, but cannot, and yet try, more enemies, and implacable ones too, than any one other thing that I know of. When such things, then, shall happen to be said at your expense, (as sometimes they certainly will,) reflect seriously upon the sentiments of uneasiness, anger, and resentment, which they excite in you; and consider whether it can be prudent, by the same means, to excite the same sentiments in others against you. It is a decided folly to lose a friend for a jest; but, in my mind, it is not a much less degree of folly, to make an enemy of an indifferent and neutral person for the sake of a *bon mot.* When things of this kind happen to be said of you, the most prudent way is to seem not to suppose that they are meant at you, but to dissemble and conceal whatever degree of anger you may feel inwardly; and should they be so plain that you cannot be supposed ignorant of their meaning, to join in the laugh of the company against yourself; acknowledge the hit to be a fair one, and the jest a good one, and play off the whole thing in seeming good-humour: but by no means reply in the same way; which only shows that you are hurt, and publishes the victory which you might have concealed. Should the thing said, indeed, injure your honour, or moral character, remember there are but two alternatives for a gentleman and a man of parts—extreme politeness, or a duel.

Avoid seeing an offront if possible.

If a man notoriously and designedly insults and affronts you, knock him down; but if he only injures you, your best revenge is to be extremely civil to him in your outward behaviour, though, at the same time, you counterwork him, and return him the compliment, perhaps with interest. This is not perfidy nor dissimulation; it would be so, if you were, at the same time, to make professions of esteem and friendship to this man; which I by no means recommend, but, on the contrary abhor. All acts of civility are, by common consent, understood to be no more than a conformity to custom, for the quiet and conveniency of society, the *agremens* of which are not to be disturbed by private dislikes and jealousies. Only women and little minds pout and spar for the entertainment of the company, that always laughs at, and never pities them. For my own part, though I would by no means give up any point to a competitor, yet I would pique myself upon showing him rather more civility than to another man. In the first place, this behaviour infallibly makes all the laughers of your side, which is a considerable party; and, in the next place, it certainly pleases the object of the competition, be it either man or woman; who never fail to say, upon such an occasion, that 'they must own you have behaved yourself very handsomely in the whole affair.'

Dissemble resentment towards enemies.

In short, let this be one invariable rule of our conduct: Never to show the least symptom of resentment, which you cannot, to a certain degree, gratify; but always to smile where you cannot strike. There would be no living in the world, if one could not conceal, and even dissemble, the just causes of resentment which one meets with every day in active and busy life. Whoever cannot master his humour should leave the world, and retire to some hermitage in an unfrequented desert. By showing an unavailing and sullen resentment, you authorize the resentment of those who can hurt you, and whom you cannot hurt; and give them that very pretence, which, perhaps, they wished for, of breaking with and injuring you; whereas the contrary behaviour would lay them under the restraints of decency, at least, and either shackle or expose their malice. Besides, captiousness, sullenness, and pouting, are most exceedingly illiberal and vulgar.

Trust not too much to any man's honesty.

Though men are all of one composition, the several ingredients are so differently proportioned in each individual, that no two are exactly alike; and no one, at all times, like himself. The ablest man will, sometimes, do weak things; the proudest man, mean things; the honestest man, ill things; and the wickedest man, good things. Study individuals, then; and if you take (as you ought to do) their outlines from their prevailing passion, suspend your last finishing strokes till you have attended to and discovered the operations of their inferior passions, appetites, and humours. A man's general character may be that of the honestest man of the world: do not dispute it; you might be thought envious or ill-natured; but, at the same time, do not take this probity upon trust to such a degree as to put your life, fortune, or reputation in his power. This honest man may happen to be your rival in power, in interest, or in love; three passions that often put honesty to most severe trials, in which it is too often cast; but, first, analyse this honest man yourself, and, then only, you will be able to judge how far you may, or may not, with safety trust him.

Study the foibles and passions of both sexes.

If you would particularly gain the affection and friendship of particular people, whether men or women, endeavour to find out their predominant excellency, if they have one, and their prevailing weakness, which every body has: and do justice to the one, and something more than justice to the other. Men have various objects in which they may excel, or at least would be thought to excel; and though they love to hear justice done to them where they know that they excel, yet they are most and best flattered upon those points where they wish to excel, and yet are doubtful whether they do or not. As for example: Cardinal Richelieu, who was undoubtedly the ablest statesman of his time, or perhaps of any other, had the idle vanity of being thought the best poet too: he envied the great Corneille his reputation, and ordered a criticism to be written upon the *Cid*. Those, therefore, who flattered skilfully, said little to him of his abilities in state affairs, or at least but *en passant*, and as it might naturally occur. But the incense which they gave him, the smoke of which they knew would turn his head in their favour, was as a *bel esprit* and a poet. Why? Because he was sure of one excellency, and distrustful as to the other.

Flatter the vanity of all.

You will easily discover every man's prevailing vanity, by observing his favourite topic of conversation; for every man talks most of what he has most a mind to be thought to excel in. Touch him but there, and you touch him to the quick.

Women have in general but one object, which is their beauty; upon which scarce any flattery is too

gross for them to swallow. Nature has hardly
formed a woman ugly enough to be insensible to
flattery upon her person. If her face is so shocking that she must, in some degree, be conscious of
it, her figure and her air, she trusts, make ample
amends for it. If her figure is deformed, her face,
she thinks, counterbalances it. If they are both
bad, she comforts herself that she has graces; a
certain manner; a *je ne sais quoi*, still more engaging than beauty. This truth is evident, from the
studied and elaborate dress of the ugliest woman
in the world. An undoubted, uncontested, conscious beauty is, of all women, the least sensible of
flattery upon that head; she knows it is her due,
and is therefore obliged to nobody for giving it her.
She must be flattered upon her understanding;
which, though she may possibly not doubt of herself, yet she suspects that men may distrust.

Do not mistake me, and think that I mean to recommend to you abject and criminal flattery: no:
flatter nobody's vices nor crimes; on the contrary,
abhor and discourage them. But there is no living
in the world without a complaisant indulgence for
people's weaknesses and innocent though ridiculous vanities. If a man has a mind to be thought
wiser and a woman handsomer than they really
are, their error is a comfortable one to themselves,
and an innocent one with regard to other people;
and I would rather make them my friends, by indulging them in it, than my enemies, by endeavouring (and that to no purpose) to undeceive them.

Suspect those who remarkably affect any one virtue.

Suspect, in general, those who remarkably affect
any one virtue; who raise it above all others, and　-

who, in a manner, intimate that they possess it exclusively: I say, suspect them; for they are commonly impostors: but do not be sure that they are always so; for I have sometimes known saints really religious, blusterers really brave, reformers of manners really honest, and prudes really chaste. Pry into the recesses of their hearts yourself, as far as you are able, and never implicitly adopt a character upon common fame; which, though generally right as to the great outlines of characters, is always wrong in some particulars.

Guard against proffered friendship.

Be upon your guard against those who, upon very slight acquaintance, obtrude their unasked and unmerited friendship and confidence upon you; for they probably cram you with them only for their own eating: but, at the same time, do not roughly reject them upon that general supposition. Examine farther, and see whether those unexpected offers flow from a warm heart and a silly head, or from a designing head and a cold heart; for knavery and folly have often the same symptoms. In the first case, there is no danger in accepting them, *valeant quantum valere possunt.* In the latter case, it may be useful to seem to accept them, and artfully to turn the battery upon him who raised it.

Disbelieve assertions by oaths.

If a man uses strong oaths or protestations to make you believe a thing which is of itself so likely and probable that the bare saying of it would be sufficient, depend upon it he lies, and is highly interested in making you believe it, or else he would not take so much pains.

Shun riotous connexions.

There is an inconsistency of friendship among young fellows who are associated by their mutual pleasures only, which has, very frequently, bad consequences. A parcel of warm hearts and unexperienced heads, heated by convivial mirth, and possibly a little too much wine, vow, and really mean at the time, eternal friendship to each other, and indiscreetly pour out their whole souls in common, and without the least reserve. These confidences are as indiscreetly repealed as they were made; for new pleasures and new places soon dissolve this ill-cemented connexion, and then very ill uses are made of these rash confidences. Bear your part, however, in young companies; nay, excel, if you can, in all the social and convivial joy and festivity that become youth. Trust them with your love-tales, if you please; but keep your serious views secret. Trust those only to some tried friend, more experienced than yourself, and who, being in a different walk of life from you, is not likely to become your rival; for I would not advise you to depend so much upon the heroic virtue of mankind, as to hope, or believe, that your competitor will ever be your friend, as to the object of that competition.

A seeming ignorance often necessary.

A seeming ignorance is very often a most necessary part of worldly knowledge. It is for instance, commonly advisable to seem ignorant of what people offer to tell you; and when they say, ' Have not you heard of such a thing?' to answer, ' No;' and to let them go on, though you know it already Some have a pleasure in telling it, because the think they tell it well; others have a pride in it, as being the sagacious discoverers; and many have a vanity in showing that they have been, though very undeservedly, trusted; all these would be disappointed, and consequently displeased, if you said, 'Yes.' Seem always ignorant (unless to one most intimate friend) of all matters of private scandal and defamation, though you should hear them a thousand times, for the parties affected always look upon the receiver to be almost as bad as the thief; and whenever they become the topic of conversation, seem to be a sceptic, though you are really a serious believer; and always take the extenuating part. But all this seeming ignorance should be joined to thorough and extensive private informations; and, indeed, it is the best method of procuring them; for most people have such a vanity in showing a superiority over others, though but for a moment, and in the merest trifles, that they will tell you what they should not, rather than not show that they can tell what you did not know; besides that such seeming ignorance will make you pass for incurious, and consequently undesigning. However, fish for facts, and take pains to be well informed of every thing that passes; but fish judiciously, and not always, nor indeed often, in the shape of direct questions; which always put people upon their guard, and, often repeated, grow tiresome. But sometimes take the things that you would know for granted; upon which somebody will, kindly and officiously, set you right; sometimes say, that you have heard so and so; and at other times seem to know more than you do, in order to know all that you want; but avoid direct questioning as much as you can.

Flexibility of manners very useful.

Human nature is the same all over the world, but its operations are so varied by education and habit, that one must see it in all its dresses, in order to be intimately acquainted with it. The passion of ambition, for instance, is the same in a courtier, a soldier, or an ecclesiastic; but, from their different educations and habits, they will take very different methods to gratify it. Civility, which is a disposition to accommodate and oblige others, is essentially the same in every country; but good breeding, as it is called, which is the manner of exerting that disposition, is different in almost every country, and merely local; and every man of sense imitates and conforms to that local good breeding of the place which he is at. A conformity and flexibility of manners is necessary in the course of the world; that is, with regard to all things which are not wrong in themselves. The *versatile ingenium* is the most useful of all. It can turn itself instantly from one object to another, assuming the proper manner for each. It can be serious with the grave, cheerful with the gay, and trifling with the frivolous.

Indeed, nothing is more engaging than a cheerful and easy conformity to people's particular manners, habits, and even weaknesses; nothing (to use a vulgar expression) should come amiss to a young fellow. He should be, for good purposes, what Alcibiades was commonly for bad ones,—a Proteus, assuming with ease, and wearing with cheerfulness, any shape. Heat, cold, luxury, abstinence, gravity, gaiety, ceremony, easiness, learning, trifling, business, and pleasure, are modes which he should be able to take, lay aside, or change occasionally, with as much ease as he would take or lay aside his hat.

Spirit.

Young men are apt to think that every thing is to be carried by spirit and vigour; that art is meanness, and that versatility and complaisance are the refuge of pusillanimity and weakness. This most mistaken opinion gives an indelicacy, an abruptness and a roughness to the manners. Fools, who can never be undeceived, retain them as long as they live; reflection with a little experience, makes men of sense shake them off soon. When they come to be a little better acquainted with themselves, and with their own species, they discover, that plain right reason is, nine times in ten, the fettered and shackled attendant of the triumph of the heart and the passions; consequently, they address themselves nine times in ten to the conqueror, not to the conquered: and conquerors, you know, must be applied to in the gentlest, the most engaging and the most insinuating manner.

But, unfortunately, young men are as apt to think themselves wise enough, as drunken men are to think themselves sober enough. They look upon spirit to be a much better thing than experience which they call coldness. They are but half mistaken; for, though spirit without experience is dangerous, experience without spirit is languid and defective. Their union, which is very rare, is perfection: you may join them, if you please; for all my experience is at your service; and I do not desire one grain of your spirit in return. Use them both, and let them reciprocally animate and check each

E

other. I mean here, by the spirit of youth only the vivacity and presumption of youth, which hinder them from seeing the difficulties or dangers of an undertaking: but I do not mean what the silly vulgar call spirit, by which they are captious, jealous of their rank, suspicious of being undervalued, and tart (as they call it) in their repartees upon the slightest occasion. This is an evil and a very silly spirit, which should be driven out, and transferred to a herd of swine.

Never neglect old acquaintance.

To conclude: never neglect or despise old, for the sake of new or more shining acquaintance ; which would be ungrateful on your part, and never forgiven on theirs. Take care to make as many personal friends, and as few personal enemies, as possible. I do not mean by personal friends, intimate and confidential friends, of which no man can hope to have half-a-dozen in the whole course of his life ; but I mean friends, in the common acceptation of the word; that is, people who speak well of you, and who would rather do you good than harm, consistently with their own interest, and no farther.

LYING.*

NOTHING is more criminal, mean, or ridiculous, than lying. It is the production either of malice,

---

* Though lies may sometimes be received for truths ; yet, after a time, their authors not only forfeit their credit, and nobody believes a word that they say, but no one can bear to hear them with patience, as being men whose words are void of all substance, and to whom no more regard ought to be paid, than if they did not speak at all, but only vented so much breath in the empty air. *Galateo.*

cowardice, or vanity; but it generally misses of its
aim in every one of these views; for lies are always
detected sooner or later. If we advance a malicious
lie in order to affect any man's fortune or character,
we may, indeed, injure him for some time, but we
shall certainly be the greatest sufferers in the end
for as soon as we are detected, we are blasted for
the infamous attempt; and whatever is said afterwards to the disadvantage of that person, however
true, passes for calumny. To lie, or to equivocate
(which is the same thing,)—to excuse ourselves for
what we have said or done, and to avoid the danger or the shame that we apprehend from it,—we
discover our fear as well as our falsehood, and only
increase, instead of avoiding, the danger and the
shame: we show ourselves to be the lowest and
meanest of mankind, and are sure to be always
treated as such. If we have the misfortune to be
in the wrong, there is something noble in frankly
owning it ; it is the only way of atoning for it, and
the only way to be forgiven. To remove a present
danger by equivocating, evading, or shuffling, is
something so despicable, and betrays so much fear,
that whoever, practises them deserves to be chas-
tised.

   There are people who indulge themselves in another sort of lying, which they reckon innocent, and
which, in one sense, is so : for it hurts nobody but
themselves : this sort of lying is the spurious
offspring of vanity begotten upon folly. These people deal in the marvellous : they have seen some
things that never existed ; they have seen other
things which they never really saw, though they
did exist, only because they were thought worth
seeing. Has any thing remarkable been said at

done in any place, or in any company, they immediately present and declare themselves eye or ear witnesses of it. They have done feats themselves, unattempted, or at least unperformed, by others. They are always the heroes of their own fables, and think that they gain consideration, or at least present attention, by it: whereas, in truth, all that they get is ridicule and contempt, not without a good degree of distrust: for one must naturally conclude, that he who will tell a lie from idle vanity, will not scruple telling a greater for interest. Had I really seen any thing so very extraordinary as to be almost incredible, I would keep it to myself, rather, than, by telling it, give any one body room to doubt for one minute of my veracity. It is most certain, that the reputation of chastity is not so necessary for a woman, as that of veracity is for a man: and with reason: for it is possible for a woman to be virtuous, though not strictly chaste; but it is not possible for a man to be virtuous, without strict veracity. The slips of the poor woman are sometimes mere bodily frailties; but a lie in a man is a vice in the mind and of the heart.

Nothing but truth can carry us through the world with either our conscience or our honour unwounded. It is not only our duty, but our interest; as a proof of which it may be observed, that the greatest fools are the greatest liars. We may safely judge of a man's truth by his degree of understanding.

DIGNITY OF MANNERS.

A CERTAIN dignity of manners is absolutely necessary to make even the most valuable character either respected or respectable in the world.

Romping, &c.

Horse-play romping, frequent and loud fits of laughter, jokes, waggery, and indiscriminate familiarity, will sink both merit and knowledge into a degree of contempt. They compose, at most, a merry fellow; and a merry fellow was never yet a respectable man. Indiscriminate familiarity either offends your superiors, or else dubs you their dependent and led captain. It gives your inferiors just, but troublesome and improper, claims of equality. A joker is near akin to a buffoon; and neither of them is the least related to wit. Whoever is admitted or sought for in company, upon any other account than that of his merit or manners, is never respected there, but only made use of. We will have Such-a-one, for he sings prettily; we will invite Such-a-one to a ball, for he dances well; we will have Such-a-one at supper, for he is always joking and laughing; we will ask another, because he plays deep at all games, or because he can drink a great deal. These are all vilifying distinctions, mortifying preferences, and exclude all ideas of esteem and regard. Whoever is *had* (as it is called) in company for the sake of any one thing singly, is singly that thing, and will never be considered in any other light, and consequently never respected, let his merits be what they will.

Pride.

Dignity of manners is not only as different from pride as true courage is from blustering, or true wit from joking, but is absolutely inconsistent with it; for nothing vilifies and degrades more than pride.*

---

* There are people so untractable in their behaviour,

The pretensions of the proud man are oftner treated
with sneer and contempt than with indignation ; as

---

that there is no possibility of conversing with them upon
any tolerable terms ; for they always run counter to the
rest of the company, or make them wait, and never cease
to incommode and be troublesome to them ; never vouch-
safing to explain their intentions, or what they would be
at. Thus, for instance, when every one else is ready to
sit down to dinner, and the table is covered ; and every
one is seated, then they, forsooth, as if they were going
to write something, will call for a pen and ink (or, perhaps, for a chamber-pot to make water) ; or will complain that they have not yet taken their morning's walk,
and pretend that it is yet time enough to go to dinner ;
and that the company must wait a little ; and wonder
what the deuce they are in such a hurry for to-day ! and
thus they put every one in confusion ; as if they alone
were of any consequence, and nothing was to be regarded
but their pleasure and convenience.

This sort of people expect also to have the preference
upon every other occasion. Wherever they go, they will
be sure to make choice of the best bed-chambers and the
softest beds : they will sit down in the principal and
most convenient place at table : in short they expect all
mankind to be solicitous to oblige them, as if they alone
were to be honoured and respected ; yet nothing pleases
them but what they themselves have contrived or executed : they ridicule others ; and at every kind of diversion,
whether in the field or in the drawing-room, a constant deference is to be paid to them by the rest of the
world.

There is another set of people, so very testy, crabbed,
and morose, that no one can ever do any thing to their
satisfaction ; and who, whatever is said to them, answer
with a frowning aspect : neither is there any end of their
chiding and reproaching their servants. And thus they
disturb a whole company with continual exclamations of
this kind : 'So! how early you called me up this morn-

we offer ridiculously too little to a tradesman who
asks ridiculously too much for his goods : but we do
not haggle with one who only asks a just and reasonable price.

Abject flattery.

Abject flattery and indiscriminate ostentation degrade, as much as indiscriminate contradiction and
noisy debate disgust : but a modest assertion of
one's own opinion, and a complaisant acquiescence
to other people's, preserve dignity.

Vulgar, low expressions, awkward motions and
address, vilify, as they imply either a very low turn
of mind, or low education and low company.

Frivolous curiosity.

Frivolous curiosity about trifles, and a laborious
attention to little objects, which neither require nor
deserve a moment's thought, lower a man, who
thence is thought (and not unjustly) incapable of

---

ing !' ' Pray look ; how cleverly you have japanned these
shoes !' ' How well you attended me to church to-day !'
' You rascal ! I have a good mind to give you my fist in
your chops ; I have, sir.' These kind of expostulations
are extremely odious and disagreeable ; and such people
ought to be avoided, as one would fly from the plague.
For though a man may be really, and in his heart, modest and humble, and may have contracted this sort of
behaviour, not so much from a bad disposition, as from
negligence and bad habit ; nevertheless, as he betrays
evident marks of pride in his external appearance, he
cannot but make himself extremely odious to mankind :
for pride is nothing less than a contempt of other people ; whereas the most insignificant person in the world
fancies himself a man of consequence, and of course entitled to respect.— Galateo.

greater matters. Cardinal de Retz very sagacious-
ly marked out Cardinal Chigi for a little mind, from
the moment that he told him he had written three
years with the same pen, and that it was an excellent good one still.

A certain degree of exterior seriousness in looks
and motions gives dignity, without excluding wit
and decent cheerfulness, which are always serious
themselves. A constant smirk upon the face, and
a whiffling activity of the body, are strong indications of futility. Whoever is in a hurry, shows that
the thing he is about is too big for him. Haste and
hurry are very different things.

To conclude: A man who has patiently been
kicked may as well pretend to courage, as a man
blasted with vices and crimes may to dignity of any
kind : but an exterior decency and dignity of manners will even keep such a man longer from sinking than otherwise he would be ; of such consequence is *decorum,* even though affected and put on.

GENTLENESS OF MANNERS WITH FIRM-NESS OR RESOLUTION OF MIND.

I do not know any one rule so unexceptionably
useful and necessary in every part of life, as to
unite *gentleness of manners* with *firmness of mind.*
The first alone would degenerate and sink into a
mean, timid complaisance and passiveness, if not
supported and dignified by the latter; which would
also deviate into impetuosity and brutality, if not
tempered and softened by the other : however, they
are seldom united. The warm, choleric man, with
strong animal spirits, despises the first, and thinks
to carry all before him by the last. He may possibly, by great accident, now and then succeed, when

he has only weak and timid people to deal with: but his general fate will be, to shock, offend, be hated, and fail. On the other hand, the cunning, crafty man thinks to gain all his ends by gentleness of manners only: *he becomes all things to all men;* he seems to have no opinion of his own, and servilely adopts the present opinion of the present person; he insinuates himself only into the esteem of fools, but is soon detected, and surely despised by every body else. The wise man (who differs as much from the cunning as from the choleric man) alone joins softness of manners with firmness of mind.

Deliver commands with mildness.

The advantages arising from an union of these qualities are equally striking and obvious. For example: if you are in authority, and have a right to command, your commands, delivered with mildness and gentleness, will be willingly, cheerfully, and consequently well, obeyed; whereas, if given brutally, they will rather be interrupted than executed. For a cool, steady resolution should show, that where you have a right to command, you will be obeyed; but, at the same time, a gentleness in the manner of enforcing that obedience should make it a cheerful one, and soften as much as possible the mortifying consciousness of inferiority.

Ask a favour with softness.

If you are to ask a favour, or even to solicit your due, you must do it with grace, or you will give those who have a mind to refuse you a pretence to do it, by resenting the manner: but, on the other hand, you must, by a steady perseverance and decent tenaciousness, show firmness and resolution.

The right motives are seldom the true ones of men's actions, especially of people in high stations, who often give to importunity and fear what they would refuse to justice or to merit. By gentleness and softness engage their hearts, if you can; at least, prevent the pretence of offence: but take care to show resolution and firmness enough to extort from their love of ease, or their fear, what you might in vain hope for from their justice or good nature. People in high life are hardened to the wants and distresses of mankind, as surgeons are to their bodily pains: they see and hear of them all day long, and even of so many simulated ones, that they do not know which are real and which not. Other sentiments are therefore to be applied to than those of mere justice and humanity; their favour must be captivated by the graces, their love of ease disturbed by unwearied importunity, or their fears wrought upon by a decent intimation of implacable cool resentment. This precept is the only way I know in the world of being loved without being despised, and feared without being hated: it constitutes the dignity of character which every wise man must endeavour to establish.

Check hastiness of temper.

To conclude: If you find that you have a hastiness in your temper, which unguardedly breaks out into indiscreet sallies or rough expressions, to either your superiors, your equals, or your inferiors, watch it narrowly, check it carefully, and call the Graces to your assistance. At the first impulse of passion, be silent, till you can be soft. Labour even to get the command of your countenance so well, that those emotions may not be read in it; a most unspeakable advantage in business! On the other hand, let no complaisance, no gentleness of temper, no weak desire of pleasing, on your part,—no wheedling, coaxing, nor flattery, on other people's, —make you recede one jot from any point that reason and prudence have bid you pursue; but return to the charge, persist, persevere, and you will find most things attainable that are possible. A yielding, timid weakness is always abused and insulted by the unjust and the unfeeling: but when sustained by firmness and resolution, is always respected commonly successful.

In your friendships and connexions, as well as in your enmities, this rule is particularly useful: let your firmness and vigour preserve and invite attachments to you; but, at the same time, let your manner hinder the enemies of your friends and dependants from becoming yours. Let your enemies be disarmed by the gentleness of your manner; but let them feel, at the same time, the steadiness of your just resentment: for there is great difference between bearing malice, which is always ungenerous, and a resolute self-defence, which is always prudent and justifiable.

Be civil, &c. to rivals or competitors.

Some people cannot gain upon themselves to be easy and civil to those who are either their rivals, competitors, or opposers, though, independantly of those accidental circumstances, they would like and esteem them. They betray a shyness and awkwardness in company with them, and catch at any little thing to expose them; and so, from temporary and only occasional opponents, make them their personal enemies. This is exceedingly weak and detrimental, as, indeed, is all humour in business; which can only be carried on successfully by unadulterated good policy and right reasoning. In such situations I would be more particularly civil, easy, and frank, with the man whose designs I traversed: this is commonly called generosity and magnanimity, but is, in truth, good sense and policy. The manner is often as important as the matter, sometimes more so: a favour may make an enemy, and an injury may make a friend, according to the different manner in which they are severally done. In fine, gentleness of manners, with firmness of mind, is a short but full description of human perfection on this side of religious and moral duties.

MORAL CHARACTER.

The moral character of a man should be not only pure, but, like Cæsar's wife, unsuspected. The least speck or blemish upon it is fatal. Nothing degrades and vilifies more; for it excites and unites detestation and contempt. There are, however, wretches in the world profligate enough to explode all notions of moral good and evil: to maintain that they are merely local, and depend entirely upon the customs and fashions of different countries: nay, there are still, if possible, more unaccountable wretches; I mean those who affect to preach and propagate such absurd and infamous notions, without believing them themselves. Avoid, as much as possible, the company of such people, who reflect a degree of discredit and infamy upon all who converse with them. But as you may sometimes, by accident fall into such company, take great care that no complaisance, no good humour, no warmth or festal mirth, ever make you seem even to acqui ence in, much less approve or applaud, such infamous doctrines. On the other hand, do not debate, nor enter into serious argument, upon a subject so much below it: but content yourself with telling them, that you know they are not serious; that you have a much better opinion of them than they would have you have; and that you are very sure they would not practise the doctrine they preach. But put your private mark upon them, and shun them for ever afterward.

There is nothing so delicate as a man's moral character, and nothing which it is his interest so much to preserve pure. Should he be suspected of injustice, malignity, perfidy, lying, &c. all the parts and knowledge in the world will never procure him esteem, friendship, or respect. I therefore recommend to you a most scrupulous tenderness for your moral character, and the utmost care not to say or do the least thing that may, ever so slightly, taint it. Show yourself, upon all occasions, the friend, but not the bully, of virtue. Even Colonel Chartres, (who was the most notorious basest rascal in the world, and who had by all sorts of crimes amassed immense wealth,) sensible of the disadvantage of a bad character, was once heard to say, that, 'altho' he would not give one farthing for virtue, he would give ten thousand pounds for a character, because he should get a hundred thousand pounds by it.' Is it possible, then that an honest man can neglect what a wise rogue would purchase so dear.

There is one of the vices above-mentioned, into which people of good education, and, in the main, of good principles, sometimes fall, from mistaken notions of skill, dexterity, and self-defence; I mean, lying; though it is inseparably attended with more

infamy and loss than any other. But I have before
given you my sentiments very freely on this subject;
I shall, therefore, conclude this head with entreat-
ing you to be scrupulously jealous of the purity of
your moral character: keep it immaculate, unblemished, unsullied, and it will be unsuspected. Defa
mation and calumny never attack where there is no
weak place; they magnify, but they do not create.

COMMON-PLACE OBSERVATIONS.

NEVER use, believe, or approve, common-place
observations. They are the common topics of wit-
lings and coxcombs: those who really have wit have
the utmost contempt for them, and scorn even to
laugh at the pert things that those would-be wits say
upon such subjects.

Religion.

Religion is one of their favourite topics: it is all
priestcraft, and an invention contrived and carried
on by priests of all religions, for their own power
and profit. From this absurd and false principle
flow the common-place insipid jokes and insults
upon the clergy. With these people, every priest
of every religion is either a public or a concealed
unbeliever, drunkard, and whoremaster; whereas,
I conceive that priests are extremely like other men,
and neither the better nor the worse for wearing a
gown or a surplice; but if they are different from
other people, probably it is rather on the side of religion and morality, or at least decency, from their
education and manner of life.*

---

* Nothing ought, on any account, to be spoken profane-
ly of God or his saints, whether seriously, or by way of

Matrimony

Another common topic for false wit and cold raillery is matrimony. Every man and his wife hate each other cordially, whatever they may pretend in public to the contrary. The husband certainly wishes his wife at the devil, and the wife certainly cuckolds her husband. Whereas I presume, that men and their wives neither love nor hate each other the more, upon account of the form of matrimony which has been said over them. The cohabitation, indeed, which is the consequence of matrimony, makes them either love or hate more accordingly as they respectively deserve it: but that would be exactly the same between any man

---

joke; however lightly some people may think of the affair, or how much pleasure soever they may take in this practice; for to speak ludicrously of the Divine being, or of things sacred, is not only the vice of the most profligate and impious rakes, but a sure indication of an ill-bred, ignorant fellow. Indeed, to hear any thing spoken irreverently of God, is so extremely shocking, that you meet with many people who on such occasions will immediately leave the room.

Nor ought we only to speak reverently of the Deity, but in all our conversations we ought to take all possible care that our words do not betray any thing loose or vicious in our lives and actions; for men detest in others those vices which even they themselves are guilty of.

In like manner, it is unpolite to talk of things unsuitable to the time when they are spoken, and to the persons who are to hear us, though the things in themselves, and when spoken in a proper place, may be really good and virtuous. A truce, therefore, with your grave discourses on sacred and religious subjects, in an assembly of young people, who are met together to be joyous and cheerful.— *Galatæo.*

and woman who lived together without being married.

Courts and cottages.

It is also a trite common-place observation, that courts are the seats of falsehood and dissimulation. That, like many, I might say most, common-place observations, is false. Falsehood and dissimulation are certainly to be found at courts; but where are they not to be found? Cottages have them, as well as courts; only with worse manners. A couple of neighbouring farmers in a village will contrive and practise as many tricks to over-reach each other at the next market, or to supplant each other in the favour of the 'squire, as any two courtiers can do, to supplant each other in the favour of their prince. Whatever poets may write, or fools believe, of rural innocence and truth, and of the perfidy of courts, this is undoubtedly true,—That shepherds and ministers are both men; their nature and passions the same, the modes of them only different.

These and many other common-place reflections upon nations or professions, in general, (which are at least as often false as true,) are the poor refuge of people who have neither wit nor invention of their own, but endeavour to shine in company by second-hand finery. I always put these pert jack-anape's out of countenance, by looking extremely grave, when they expect that I should laugh at their pleasantries; and by saying, ' Well, and so?' as if they had not done, and that the sting were still to come. This disconcerts them ; as they have no resources in themselves, and have but one set of jokes to live upon. Men of parts are not reduced to these shifts, and have the utmost contempt for them : they find proper subjects enough for either useful

or lively conversation; they can be witty without
satire or common-place, and serious without being
dull.

ORATORY.

ORATORY, or the art of speaking well, is useful in
every situation of life, and absolutely necessary in
most. A man cannot distinguish himself without
it, in parliament, in the pulpit, or at the bar; and
even in common conversation, he who has acquired
an easy and habitual eloquence, and who speaks
with propriety and accuracy, will have a great advantage over those who speak inelegantly and in-
correctly. The business of oratory is to persuade;
and to please is the most effectual step towards persuading. It is very advantageous for a man who
speaks in public, to please his hearers so much as
to gain their attention; which he cannot possibly
do without the assistance of oratory.

It is certain, that by study and application every
man may make himself a tolerably good orator;
eloquence depending upon observation and care.
Every man may, if he pleases, make choice of good
instead of bad words and phrases, may speak with
propriety instead of impropriety, and may be clear
and perspicuous in his recitals, instead of dark and
unintelligible; he may have grace instead of awkwardness in his gestures and déportment: in short,
it is in the power of every man, with pains and application, to be a very agreeable, instead of a very
disagreeable, speaker; and it is well worth the labour to excel other men in that particular article in
which they excel beasts.

Demosthenes thought it so essentially necessary
to speak well, that, though he naturally stuttered,

and had weak lungs, he resolved, by application, to
overcome those disadvantages. He cured his stam-
mering by putting small pebbles in his mouth; and
gradually strengthened his lungs, by daily using
himself to speak loudly and distinctly for a considerable time. In stormy weather he often visited
the sea-shore, where he spoke as loud as he could,
in order to prepare himself for the noise and mur-
murs of the popular assemblies of the Athenians,
before whom he was to speak. By this extraordinary care and attention, and the constant study of
the best authors, he became the greatest orator that
his own or any other age or country has produced.

Whatever language a person uses, he should
speak it in its greatest purity, and according to the
rules of grammar: nor is it sufficient that we do not
speak a language ill, we must endeavour to speak
it well; for which purpose, we should read the best
authors with attention, and observe how people of
fashion and education speak. Common people, in
general, speak ill; they make use of inelegant and
vulgar expressions, which people of rank never do.
In numbers, they frequently join the singular and
the plural together, and confound the masculine
with the feminine gender, and seldom make choice
of the proper tense. To avoid all these faults, we
should read with attention, and observe the turn
and expressions of the best authors; nor should we
pass over a word we do not perfectly understand,
without searching or inquiring for the exact meaning of it.

It is said that a man must be born a poet, but it
is in his power to make himself an orator; for, to
be a poet, requires a certain degree of strength and
vivacity of mind; but attention, reading, and labour, are sufficient to form an orator.

PEDANTRY.

Every excellency, and every virtue, has its kindred vice or weakness; and if carried beyond certain bounds, sinks into the one or the other. Generosity often runs into profusion, economy into avarice, courage into rashness, caution into timidity, and so on;—insomuch that, I believe, there is more judgment required for the proper conduct of our virtues, than for avoiding their opposite vices. Vice, in its true light, is so deformed, that it shocks at first sight; and would hardly ever seduce us, if it did not, at first, wear the mask of some virtue. But virtue is, in itself, so beautiful, that it charms us at first sight; engages us more and more, upon farther acquaintance; and, as with other beauties, we think excess impossible: it is here that judgment is necessary to moderate and direct the effects of an excellent cause. In the same manner, great learning, if not accompanied with sound judgment, frequently carries us into error, pride, and pedantry.

Never pronounce arbitrarily.

Some learned men, proud of their knowledge, only speak to decide, and give judgment without appeal; the consequence of which is, that mankind, provoked by the insult, and injured by the oppression, revolt; and, in order to shake off the tyranny, even call the lawful authority in question. The more you know, the modester you should be; and that modesty is the surest way of gratifying your vanity. Even where you are sure, seem rather doubtful; represent, but do not pronounce; and, if you would convince others, seem open to conviction yourself.

Affect not to prefer the ancients to moderns.

Others, to show their learning, or often from the prejudices of a school-education, where they hear of nothing else, are always talking of the ancients as something more than men, and of the moderns as something less. They are never without a classic or two in their pockets; they stick to the old good sense; they read none of the modern trash; and will show you plainly, that no improvement has been made, in any one art or science, these last seventeen hundred years. I would by no means have you disown your acquaintance with the ancients; but still less would I have you brag of an exclusive intimacy with them. Speak of the moderns without contempt, and of the ancients without idolatry; judge them all by their merits, but not by their ages; and if you happen to have an Elzevir classic in your pocket, neither show it nor mention it.

Reason not from ancient authenticity.

Some great scholars, most absurdly, draw all their maxims, both for public and private life, from what they call parallel cases in the ancient authors; without considering, that, in the first place, there never were, since the creation of the world, two cases exactly parallel! and, in the next place, that there never was a case stated, or even known, by any historian, with every one of its circumstances; which, however, ought to be known, in order to be reasoned from. Reason upon the case itself, and the several circumstances that attend it, and act accordingly; but not from the authority of ancient poets or historians. Take into your consi-

deration, if you please, cases seemingly analogous;
but take them as helps only, not as guides.

Abstain from learned ostentation.

There is another species of learned men, who,
though less dogmatical and supercilious, are not
less impertinent. These are the communicative
and shining pedants, who adorn their conversation,
even with women, by happy quotations of Greek
and Latin, and who have contracted such a familiarity with the Greek and Roman authors, that they
call them by certain names or epithets denoting intimacy; as *old* Homer; that *sly rogue* Horace;
Maro, instead of Virgil; *Naso,* instead of Ovid.
These are often imitated by coxcombs who have no
learning at all; but who have got some names and
some scraps of ancient authors by heart, which they
improperly and impertinently retail in all companies, in hopes of passing for scholars. If, therefore, you would avoid the accusation of pedantry
on one hand, or the suspicion of ignorance on the
other, abstain from learned ostentation. Speak the
language of the company you are in; speak it purely, and unlarded with any other. Never seem
wiser nor more learned than the people you are
with. Wear your learning, like your watch, in a
private pocket; and do not pull it out, and strike
it, merely to show that you have one. If you are
asked what o'clock it is, tell it; but do not proclaim
it hourly and unasked, like the watchman.

PLEASURE.

Many young people adopt pleasures, for which
they have not the least taste, only because they are
called by that name. They often mistake so total-

ly, as to imagine that debauchery is pleasure.
Drunkenness, which is equally destructive to body
and mind, is certainly a fine pleasure! Gaming,
which draws us into a thousand scrapes, leaves us
pennyless, and gives us the air and manners of an
outrageous madman, is another most exquisite
pleasure!

Pleasure is the rock which most young people
split upon; they launch out with crowded sails in
quest of it, but without a compass to direct their
course, or reason sufficient to steer the vessel;
therefore pain and shame, instead of pleasure, are
the returns of their voyage.

A man of pleasure, in the vulgar acceptation of
that phrase, means only a beastly drunkard, an
abandoned rake, and a profligate swearer. We
should weigh the present enjoyment of our pleasures against the unavoidable consequences of
them, and then let our common sense determine
the choice.

We may enjoy the pleasures of the table and
wine, but stop short of the pains inseparably annexed to an excess in either. We may let other
people do as they will, without formally and sen-
tentiously rebuking them for it; but we must be
firmly resolved not to destroy our own faculties and
constitution, in compliance to those who have no
regard to their own. We may play to give us pleasure, but not to give us pain; we play for trifles in
mixed companies, to amuse ourselves and conform
to custom. Good company are not fond of having
a man reeling drunk among them; nor is it agreeable to see another tearing his hair and blasphe-
ming, for having lost, at play, more than he is able
to pay; or a rake, with half a nose, crippled by

coarse and infamous debauches. Those who practise and brag of these things make no part of good company; and are most unwillingly, if ever, admitted into it. A real man of fashion and pleasure observes decency; at least, he neither borrows nor affects vices: and if he is so unfortunate as to have any, he gratifies them with choice, delicacy, and secrecy.

We should be as attentive to our pleasures as to our studies. In the latter, we should observe and reflect upon all we read; and, in the former, be watchful and attentive to every thing we see and hear; and let us never have it to say, as some fools do, of things that were said and done before their faces, ' That indeed they did not mind them, because they were thinking of something else.' Why were they thinking of something else? And if they were, why did they come there? Wherever we are, we should (as it is vulgarly expressed) have our ears and our eyes about us. We should listen to every thing that is said, and see every thing that is done. Let us observe without being thought observers; for otherwise people will be upon their guard before us.

All gaming, field-sports, and such other amusements, where neither the understanding nor the senses have the least share, are frivolous, and the resources of little minds, who either do not think or do not love to think. But the pleasures of a man of parts either flatter the senses or improve the mind.

There are liberal and illiberal pleasures, as well as liberal and illiberal arts. Sottish drunkenness, indiscriminate gluttony, driving coaches, rustic sports, such as fox chases, horse races, &c. are infinitely below the honest and industrious professions of a tailor and shoe maker.

The more we apply to business, the more we relish our pleasures : the exercise of the mind in the morning, by study, whets the appetite for the pleasures of the evening, as the exercise of the body whets the appetite for dinner. Business and pleasure rightly understood, mutually assist each other, instead of being enemies, as foolish or dull people often think them. We cannot taste pleasures truly, unless we earn them by previous business ; and few people do business well, who do nothing else. But when I speak of pleasures, I always mean the elegant pleasures of a rational being, and not the brutal ones of swine.

PREJUDICES.

NEVER adopt the notions of any books you may read, or of any company you may keep, without examining whether they are just or not; as you will otherwise be liable to be hurried away by prejudices, instead of being guided by reason, and quietly cherish error, instead of seeking for truth.

Use and assert your own reason; reflect, examine, and analyse, every thing, in order to form a sound and mature judgment; let no *ipse dixit* impose upon your understanding, mislead your actions, or dictate your conversation. Be early what, if you are not, you will, when too late, wish you had been. Consult your reason betimes : I do not say that it will always prove an unerring guide, for human reason is not infallible; but it will prove the least erring guide that you can follow. Books and conversation may assist it; but adopt neither blindly and implicitly : try both by that best rule, which

God has given to direct us,—reason. Of all the troubles, do not decline, as many people do, that of thinking. The herd of mankind can hardly be said to think; their notions are almost all adoptive; and, in general, I believe it is better that it should be so; as such common prejudices contribute more to order and quiet, than their own separate reasonings would do, uncultivated and unimproved as they are.

Local prejudices prevail only with the herd of mankind, and do not impose upon cultivated, informed, and reflecting minds: but then there are notions equally false, though not so glaringly absurd, which are entertained by people of superior and improved understandings, merely for want of the necessary pains to investigate, the proper attention to examine, and the penetration requisite to determine, the truth. Those are the prejudices which I would have you guard against by a manly exertion and attention of your reasoning faculty

RELIGION.

ERRORS and mistakes, however gross, in matters of opinion, if they are sincere, are to be pitied, but not punished nor laughed at. The blindness of the understanding is as much to be pitied as the blindness of the eyes; and it is neither laughable nor criminal for a man to lose his way in either case. Charity bids us endeavour to set him right, by arguments and persuasions, but charity, at the same time, forbids us either to punish or ridicule his misfortune. Every man seeks for truth, but God only knows who has found it. It is unjust to persecute and absurd to ridicule people for their several opinions, which they cannot help entertaining

F

upon the conviction of their reason. It is he who tells or acts a lie that is guilty, and not he who honestly and sincerely believes the lie.

The object of all public worships in the world is the same; it is that great Eternal Being who created every thing. The different manners of worship are by no means subjects of ridicule. Each sect thinks his own the best; and I know no infallible judge in this world to decide which is the best.

EMPLOYMENT OF TIME.

How little do we reflect on the use and value of time! It is in every body's mouth, but in few people's practice. Every fool, who slatterns away his whole time in nothings, frequently utters some trite common-place sentence to prove, at once, the value and the fleetness of time. The sun dials, all over Europe, have some ingenious inscription to that effect; so that nobody squanders away their time without frequently hearing and seeing how necessary it is to employ it well, and how irrecoverable it is if lost. Young people are apt to think they have so much time before them, that they may squander what they please of it, and yet have enough left; as great fortunes have frequently seduced people to a ruinous profusion. But all these admonitions are useless, where there is not a fund of good sense and reason to suggest rather than receive them.

Idleness.

Time is precious, life short, and consequently not a single moment should be lost. Sensible men know how to make the most of time, and put out their whole sum either to interest or pleasure: they are never

idle, but continually employed either in amusements or study. It is an universal maxim, that
idleness is the mother of vice. It is, however, certain, that laziness is the inheritance of fools, and
nothing can be so despicable as a sluggard. Cato,
the censor, a wise and virtuous Roman, used to
say, there were but three actions of his life that he
regretted : the first was, the having revealed a secret to his wife ; the second, that he had once gone
by sea when he might have gone by land ; and the
third, the having passed one day without *doing any
thing.*

Reading.

‘ Take care of the pence; for the pounds will
take care of themselves;’ was a very just and sensible reflection of old Mr. Lowndes, the famous secretary of the Treasury under William III., Anne,
and George I. I therefore recommend to you to
take care of minutes ; for hours will take care of
themselves. Be doing something or other all day
long; and not neglect half-hours, and quarters of
hours, which, at the year’s end, amount to a great
sum, For instance : there are many short intervals in the day, between studies and pleasures ; instead of sitting idle and yawning, in those intervals,
snatch up some valuable book, and continue the
reading of that book till you have got through it :
never burden your mind with more than one thing
at a time; and, in reading this book, do not run
over it superficially, but read every passage twice
over, at least ; do not pass on to a second, till you
thoroughly understand the first, nor quit the book
till you are master of the subject; for unless you do
this, you may read it through, and not remember

the contents of it for a week. The books I would particularly recommend, amongst others, are the Marchioness Lambert's Advice to her Son and Daughter, Cardinal Retz's Maxims, Rochefoucault's Moral Reflections, Bruyere's Characters, Fontenelle's Plurality of Worlds, Sir Josiah Child on Trade, Bolingbroke's Works : for style, his Remarks on the History of England, under the name of Sir John Oldcastle ; Puffendorf's Jus Gentium, and Grotius de Jure Belli et Pacis : the last two are well translated by Barbeyrac. For occasional half hours or less, read works of invention, wit, and humour: but never waste your minutes on trifling authors, either ancient or modern.

Nor are pleasures idleness or time lost, provided they are the pleasures of a rational being: on the contrary, a certain portion of time employed in those pleasures is very usefully employed.

Transacting business.

Whatever business you have, do it the first moment you can ; never by halves, but finish it without interruption, if possible. Business must not be sauntered and trifled with ; and you must not say to it, as Felix did to Paul, ' At a more convenient season I will speak to thee.' The most convenient season for business is the first ; but study and business, in some measure, point out their own times to a man of sense ; time is much oftener squandered away in the wrong choice and improper methods of amusement and pleasures.

Method.

Dispatch is the soul of business ; and nothing contributes more to dispatch than method. Lay down

a method for every thing, and stick to it inviolably,
as far as unexpected incidents may allow. Fix one
certain hour and day in the week for your accounts,
and keep them together in their proper order; by
which means they will require very little time, and
you can never be much cheated. Whatever letters
and papers you keep, docket and tie them up in
their respective classes, so that you may instantly
have recourse to any one. Lay down a method also for your reading, for which you allot a certain
share of your mornings; let it be in a consistent and
consecutive course, and not in that desultory and
immethodical manner, in which many people read
scraps of different authors upon different subjects.
Keep a useful and short common-place book of what
you read, to help your memory only, and not for
pedantic quotations. Never read history without
having maps, and a chronological book or tables
lying by you, and constantly recurred to; without
which, history is only a confused heap of facts.

You will say, it may be, as many young people
would, that all this order and method is very troublesome, only fit for dull people, and a disagreeable
restraint upon the noble spirit and fire of youth.
I deny it; and assert, on the contrary, that it will
procure you both more time and more taste for
your pleasures; and, so far from being troublesome
to you, that, after you have pursued it a month, it
would be troublesome to you to lay it aside. Business whets the appetite, and gives a taste to pleasures, as exercise does to food; and business can
never be done without method: it raises the spirits
for pleasures: and a *spectacle*, a ball, an assembly,
will much more sensibly affect a man who has employed, than a man who has lost the preceding part

of the day; nay, I will venture to say, that a fine lady will seem to have more charms to a man of study or business than to a saunterer. The same listlessness runs through his whole conduct; and he is as insipid in his pleasures, as inefficient in every thing else.

I hope you earn your pleasures, and consequently taste them; for, by the way, I know a great many men who call themselves men of pleasure, but who, in truth, have none. They adopt other people's indiscriminately, but without any taste of their own. I have known them often inflict excesses upon themselves, because they thought them genteel; though they sat as awkwardly upon them as other people's clothes would have done. Have no pleasures but your own, and then you will shine in them.

Many people think that they are in pleasures provided they are neither in study nor in business. Nothing like it; they are doing nothing, and might just as well be asleep. They contract habitudes from laziness, and they only frequent those places where they are free from all restraints and attentions. Be upon your guard against this idle profusion of time; and let every place you go to be either the scene of quick and lively pleasures, or the school of your improvements; let every company you go into, either gratify your senses, extend your knowledge, or refine your manners.

If, by accident, two or three hours are sometimes wanting for some useful purpose, borrow them from your sleep. Six, or at most seven, hours sleep is, for a constancy, as much as you or any body can want: more is only laziness and dozing, and is both unwholesome and stupifying. If, by chance, your business or your pleasures should keep you up till four or five o'clock in the morning, rise exactly at your usual time, that you may not lose the precious morning hours; and that the want of sleep may force you to go to bed earlier the next night.

Guard against frivolousness.

Above all things, guard against frivolousness. The frivolous mind is always busied, but to little purpose: it takes little objects for great ones, and throws away upon trifles that time and attention which only important things deserve. Nicknacks, butterflies, shells, insects, &c. are the objects of their most serious researches. They contemplate the dress, not the characters of the company they keep. They attend more to the decorations of a play, than to the sense of it; and to the ceremonies of a court, more than to its politics. Such an employment of time is an absolute loss of it.

To conclude this subject: sloth, indolence, and effeminacy, are pernicious, and unbecoming a young fellow; let them be your resource forty years hence at soonest. Determine, at all events, and however disagreeable it may be to you in some respects, and for some time, to keep the most distinguished and fashionable company of the place you are at, either for their rank or for their learning, or le bel esprit et le gout. This gives you credentials to the best companies, whosever you go afterward.

Know the true value of time; snatch, seize, and enjoy, every moment of it. No idleness, no laziness, no procrastination; never put off till to-morrow what you can do to-day. That was the rule of the famous and unfortunate pensionary De Witt; who, by strictly following it, found time not only to

do the whole business of the republic, but to pass
his evenings at assemblies and suppers, as if he had
nothing else to do or think of.

VANITY.

BE extremely on your guard against vanity, the
common failing of inexperienced youth; but particularly against that kind of vanity that dubs a man
a coxcomb; a character which, once acquired, is
more indelible than that of priesthood.   It is not to
be imagined by how many different ways vanity
defeats its own purposes.   One man decides pe-
remptorily upon every subject, betrays his ignorance upon many, and shows a disgusting presumption upon the rest; another desires to appear successful among the women : he hints at the encou
ragement he has received from those of the most
distinguished rank and beauty, and intimates a particular connexion with some one; if it is true, it is
ungenerous; if false, it is infamous; but, in either
case, he destroys the reputation he wants to get.
Some flatter their vanity by little extraneous objects, which have not the least relation to themselves; such as being descended from, related to,
or acquainted with, people of distinguished merit
and eminent characters.   They talk perpetually of
their grandfather Such-a-one, their uncle Such-a-
one, whom, possibly, they are hardly acquainted
with.   But admitting it all to be as they would have
it, what then? Have they the more merit for those
accidents? Certainly not.   On the contrary, their
taking up adventitious, proves their want of intrin-
sic merit; a rich man never borrows.   Take this
rule for granted, as a never failing one, that you
must never seem to affect the character in which

you have a mind to shine. Modesty is the only sure
bait, when you angle for praise. The affectation
of courage will make even a brave man pass only for
a bully; as the affectation of wit will make a man
of parts pass for a coxcomb. By this modesty
I do not mean timidity and awkward bashfulness.
On the contrary, be inwardly firm and steady;
know your own value, whatever it may be, and
act upon that principle; but take great care to
let nobody discover that you do know your own
value. Whatever real merit you have, other people will discover; and people always magnify
their own discoveries, as they lessen those of others.

VIRTUE.

VIRTUE is a subject which deserves your and
every man's attention. It consists in doing good
and in speaking truth; the effects of it, therefore,
are advantageous to all mankind, and to one's self
in particular. Virtue makes us pity and relieve the
misfortunes of mankind; it makes us promote justice and good order in society; and, in general, contributes to whatever tends to the real good of mankind. To ourselves it gives an inward comfort and
satisfaction, which nothing else can do, and which
nothing else can rob us of. All other advantages
depend upon others, as much as upon ourselves.
Riches, power, and greatness, may be taken away
from us by the violence and injustice of others, or
by inevitable accidents; but virtue depends only
upon ourselves, and nobody can take it away from
us. Sickness may deprive us of all the pleasures
of the body; but it cannot deprive us of our virtue,
nor of the satisfaction which we feel from it. A
virtuous man, under all the misfortunes of life, still

finds an inward comfort and satisfaction, which make him happier than any wicked man can be with all the other advantages of life. If a man has acquired great power and riches by falsehood, injustice, and oppression, he cannot enjoy them, because his conscience will torment him, and constantly reproach him with the means by which he got them. The stings of his conscience will not even let him sleep quietly, but he will dream of his crimes; and, in the day-time, when alone, and when he has time to think, he will be uneasy and melancholy. He is afraid of every thing; for, as he knows mankind must hate him, he has reason to think they will hurt him if they can. Whereas, if a virtuous man be ever so poor and unfortunate in the world, still his virtue is its own reward, and will comfort him under all afflictions. The quiet and satisfaction of his conscience make him cheerful by day and sleep sound at nights: he can be alone with pleasure, and is not afraid of his own thoughts. Virtue forces her way, and shines through the obscurity of a retired life; and, sooner or later, it always is rewarded.

To conclude:—Lord Shaftesbury says, that he would be virtuous for his own sake, though nobody were to know it; as he would be clean for his own sake, though nobody were to see him.

USEFUL

MISCELLANEOUS OBSERVATIONS

ON

MEN AND MANNERS.

SELECTED FROM LORD CHESTERFIELD'S LETTERS.

—⊕⊘⊕—

A MAN who does not solidly establish, and really deserve, a character of truth, probity, good manners, and good morals, at his first setting out in the world, may impose, and shine like a meteor for a very short time, but will very soon vanish and be extinguished with contempt. People easily pardon in young men the common irregularities of the senses; but they do not forgive the least vice of the heart.

The greatest favours may be done so awkwardly and bunglingly as to offend; and disagreeable things may be done so agreeably as almost to oblige.

There are very few captains of foot who are not much better company than ever Descartes or Sir Isaac Newton were. I honour and respect such superior geniuses; but I desire to converse with people of this world, who bring into company their share, at least of cheerfulness, good breeding, and knowledge of mankind. In common life, one much oftener wants small money and silver than gold.— Give me a man who has ready cash about him for present expenses; sixpences, shillings, half-crowns, and crowns, which circulate easily: but a man who has only an ingot of gold about him, is much above common purposes, and his riches are not handy nor convenient. Have as much gold as you please in one pocket, but take care always to keep change in the other; for you will much oftener have occasion for a shilling than for a guinea.

Advice is seldom welcome; and those who want it the most, always like it the least.

Envy is one of the meanest and most tormenting of all passions, as there is hardly a person existing that has not given uneasiness to an envious breast; for the envious man cannot be happy while he beholds others so

A great action will always meet with the approbation of mankind, and the inward pleasure which it produces is not to be expressed.

Humanity is the particular characteristic of great minds: little, vicious minds abound with anger and revenge, and are incapable of feeling the exalted pleasure of forgiving their enemies.

The ignorant and the weak only are idle; those who have acquired a good stock of knowledge always desire to increase it. Knowledge is like power in this respect,—that those who have the most are most desirous of having more. Idleness is only the refuge of weak minds and the holiday of fools.

Every man has a natural right to his liberty; and whoever endeavours to ravish it from him, deserves death more than the robber who attacks us for our money on the highway.

Modesty is a commendable quality, and generally accompanies true merit: it engages and captivates the minds of people; for nothing is more shocking and disgustful than presumption and impudence. A man is despised who is always commending himself, and who is the hero of his own story.

Not to perform our promise, is a folly, a dishonour, and a crime. It is a folly, because no one will rely on us afterwards; and it is a dishonour and a crime, because truth is the first duty of religion and morality: and whoever is not possessed of truth cannot be supposed to have any one good quality, and must be held in detestation by all good men.

Wit may create many admirers, but makes few friends. It shines and dazzles, like the noon-day sun; but, like that too, is very apt to scorch, and therefore is always feared. The milder morning and evening light and heat of that planet soothe and calm our minds. Never seek for wit: if it presents itself, well and good; but even in that case let your judgment interpose; and take care that it be not at the expense of any body. Pope says very truly,

' There are whom heaven has blest with store of wit,
Yet want as much again to govern it.'

And in another place, I doubt with too much truth,

' For wit and judgment ever are at strife,
Though meant each other's aid, like man and wife.'

A proper secrecy is the only mystery of able men; mystery is the only secrecy of weak and cunning men.

To tell any friend, wife, or mistress, any secret with which they have nothing to do, is discovering to them such an unretentive weakness, as must convince them that you will tell it to twenty others, and consequently that they may reveal it without the risk of being discovered. But a secret properly communicated, only to those who are to be concerned in the question, will probably be kept by them, though they should be a good many. Little secrets are commonly told again, but great ones generally kept.

A man who tells nothing, or who tells all, will equally have nothing told him.

If a fool knows a secret, he tells it because he is a fool ; if a knave knows one, he tells it wherever it is his interest to tell it. But women and young men are very apt to tell what secrets they know, from the vanity of having been trusted. Trust none of these, wherever you can help it.

In your friendships, and in your enmities, let your confidence, and your hostilities have certain bounds ; make not the former dangerous, nor the latter irreconcilable. There are strange vicissitudes in business

Smoothe your way to the head through the heart. The way of reason is a good one ; but it is commonly something longer, and perhaps not so sure.

Spirit is now a very fashionable word : To act with spirit, to speak with spirit, means only to act rashly, and to talk indiscreetly. An able man shows his spirit by gentle words and resolute actions ; he is neither hot nor timid.

Patience is a most necessary qualification for business ; many a man would rather you heard his story than granted his request. One must seem to hear the unreasonable demands of the petulant unmoved, and the tedious details of the dull untired. This is the least price that a man must pay for a high station.

It is always right to detect a fraud, and to perceive a folly ; but it is often very wrong to expose either. A man of business should always have his eyes open, but must often seem to have them shut.

In courts (and every where else) bashfulness and timidity are as prejudicial on one hand, as impudence and rashness are on the other. A steady assurance and a cool intrepidity, with an exterior modesty, are the true and necessary medium.

Never apply for what you see very little probability of obtaining; for you will, by asking improper and unattainable things, accustom the ministers to refuse you so often, that they will find it easy to refuse you the properest and most reasonable ones. It is a common but a most mistaken rule at court, to ask for every thing in order to get something: you do get something by it, it is true; but that something is refusals and ridicule. This maxim, like the former, is of general application.

A cheerful, easy countenance and behaviour are very useful: they make fools think you a good-natured man, and they make designing men think you an undesigning one.

There are some occasions in which a man must tell half his secret, in order to conceal the rest; but there is seldom one in which a man should tell it all. Great skill is necessary to know how far to go, and where to stop.

Ceremony is necessary, as the out-work and defence of manners.

A man's own good breeding is his best security against other people's ill manners.

Good breeding carries along with it a dignity that is respected by the most petulant. Ill breeding invites and authorizes the familiarity of the most timid. No man ever said a pert thing to the Duke of Marlborough. No man ever said a civil one (though many a flattering one) to Sir Robert Walpole.

Knowledge may give weight, but accomplishments only give lustre; and many more people see than weigh.

Most arts require long study and application; but the most useful art of all, that of pleasing, requires only the desire.

It is to be presumed, that a man of common sense who does not desire to please, desires nothing at all; since he must know that he cannot obtain any thing without it.

A skilful negociator will most carefully distinguish between the little and the great objects of his business, and will be as frank and open in the former, as he will be secret and pertinacious in the latter.—This maxim holds equally true in common life.

The Duc de Sully observes very justly, in his Memoirs, that nothing contributed more to his rise, than that prudent economy which he had observed from his youth; and by which he had always a sum of money before-hand, in case of emergencies.

It is very difficult to fix the particular point of economy: the best error of the two is on the parsimonious side: that may be corrected, the other cannot.

The reputation of generosity is to be purchased pretty cheap; it does not depend so much upon a man's general expense, as it does upon his giving handsomely where it is proper to give at all. A man, for instance, who should give a servant four shillings, would pass for covetous, while he who gave him a crown would be reckoned generous; so that the difference of those two opposite characters turns upon one shilling. A man's character in that particular depends a great deal upon the report of his own servants; a mere trifle above common wages makes their report favourable.

Take care always to form your establishment so much within your income, as to leave a sufficient fund for unexpected contingencies and a prudent liberality. There is hardly a year in any man's life in which a small sum of ready money may not be employed to great advantage.

END OF 'LORD CHESTERFIELD'S ADVICE TO HIS SON.'

SUPPLEMENT,

CONTAINING

EXTRACTS FROM VARIOUS BOOKS,

RECOMMENDED BY

LORD CHESTERFIELD

TO

MR. STANHOPE.*

TO WHICH ARE ADDED,

THE POLITE PHILOSOPHER;

Or, An Essay on the Art which makes a Man happy in
himself, and agreeable to others:

DR. BLAIR'S ADVICE TO YOUTH,

DR. FORDYCE ON HONOUR AS A PRINCIPLE;

LORD BURGHLEY'S TEN PRECEPTS TO
HIS SON;

DR. FRANKLIN'S WAY TO WEALTH;

AND

POPE'S UNIVERSAL PRAYER.

---

* See Page 118.

ADVICE

OF

A MOTHER TO HER SON:

BY THE

MARCHIONESS DE LAMBERT.

A Tract particularly recommended to his Son by Lord Chesterfield.

—◦◦◦—

WHATEVER care is used in the education of children, it is still too little to answer the end; to make it succeed, there must be excellent governors; but where shall we find them, when princes find it difficult to get and keep them for themselves? Where can we meet with men so much superior to others, as to deserve to be intrusted with their conduct? Yet the first years of a man's life are precious, since they lay the foundation of the merit of the rest.

There are but two seasons of life in which truth distinguishes itself for our advantage: in youth, for our instruction; and in our advanced years, to comfort us. In the age that passions reign, truth generally quits us for the time.

Two celebrated men,* out of their friendship to me, have had the care of your education; but as

---

* P. Boubours and P. Cheminais.

they were obliged to follow the method of studies
settled in colleges, they applied themselves more in
your early youth to improve your mind with learning, than to make you know the world, or instruct
you in the decorum of life.

I am going, my son, to give you some precepts
for the conduct of yours; read them without thinking it a trouble. They are not dry lectures, that
carry the air of a mother's authority: they are rather the advice of a friend, and have this merit,
that they come from my heart.

At your entering the world, you must certainly
propose to yourself some end or other : you have
too much sense to care to live without any design at
all ; nor can you aspire to any thing more becoming and worthy of you than glory. It is a noble
view for you to entertain ; but it is fit for you to
know what is meant by the term, and what notion
you frame of it.

It is of various kinds, and each profession has a
glory that is peculiar to it. In yours, my son, it
means the glory that attends valour. This is the
glory of heroes; it makes a brighter figure than any
other ; it always carries with it the true marks of
honour and the recompenses it deserves: Fame
seems to have no tongue but to sound their praise ;
and when you arrive at a certain degree of reputation, every thing you do is considerable. All the
world has agreed to give the pre-eminence to military virtues ; it is no more than their due. They
cost dear enough ; but there are several ways of
discharging their obligation.

Some engage in the profession of arms, merely
to avoid the shame of degenerating from their ancestors; others follow it not only out of duty, but

inclination. The first scarce ever raise themselves
above their rank in the world ; it is a debt they pay,
and they go no farther.   The others, flushed with
hopes, and carried on by ambition, march a giant's
pace in the road of glory.   Some purpose only to
make their fortune ; others have their advancement
and immortality itself in view. Such as stint themselves to the making a fortune, never have a very
extensive merit. A man that does not aim at raising to himself a great name, will never perform any
great actions. And such as go carelessly on in the
road of their professions suffer all the fatigues, without acquiring either the honour or recompense that
naturally attend it.

If people understood their own interest rightly,
they would not lay a stress upon raising a fortune,
but would, in all professions, have their glory and
reputation in view.   When you attain to a certain
degree of merit, (and it is generally known,) the
great glory and reputation you have acquired never
fail to make your fortune. A man cannot have too
much ardour to distinguish himself, nor can his desires of advancement be encouraged by hopes that
are too flattering.

There must be great views to give a great vigour
to the soul ; it is not easy otherwise to make it exert
itself. Let your love of glory be ever so eager and
active, you may still fall short of your aim ; yet,
though you should advance but half way, it is always glorious to have dared.

There is nothing so improper for a young man, as
that modesty which makes him fancy he is not capable of great things. This modesty is a faintness
of soul, which hinders it from exerting itself, and
running with a swift career towards glory. Agesi-

laus was told that the king of Persia was the greatest king. 'Why should he be greater than I,' replied he, 'so long as I have a sword by my side?'
There is a superior genius and merit in some
persons, that tells them nothing is impossible for
them.

Fortune, my son, did not level your way to glory:
to make it easier for you, I gave you a regiment betimes; being persuaded that there is no entering
too soon into a profession where experience is so
necessary, and that the first years of a man's life
lay the foundation of his character, and enable the
world to judge of his future conduct in the residue
of it. You made the campaign of Barcelona, the
most successful to the king's troops, and yet the
least celebrated of any. You return into Italy,
where every thing is against us; where we are to
fight not only with the enemy, but the climate, the
situation and prejudices of the country. Campaigns
that are unhappy for the king, prove so likewise for
private men; the corpses of the dead, and the
faults of the living, are buried in one common
grave: Fame is hushed, and has nothing to say of
the service of such as are left: but you may still
depend upon it, that true valour is never unknown.
There are so many eyes observing your behaviour,
that you can never want as many witnesses of
your worth: besides, you learn more in such campaigns; you try your own abilities; you know yourself well enough to judge what you can do upon occasion; others know it too; and if you do not raise
yourself a reputation in a moment, you are sure to
gain one in the end.

Great names are not formed in a day; nor is it
valour alone that makes extraordinary men: she

begins, indeed, to form them, but other virtues must concur to finish them.

The notion of a hero is inconsistent with the character of a man without justice, probity, and magnanimity. It is not enough to have a name for your valour; you must have a name likewise for your probity. All the virtues must unite together to form a hero. Valour, my son, is not to be inspired by advice; it is a gift of nature: but such a one that a person may possess it in the highest degree, and yet deserve very little esteem in other respects.

The generality of young men fancy they are obliged to nothing else, when once they have acquired the military virtues; and that they are allowed to be unjust, rude and unmannerly. Do not carry the prerogative of the sword too far; it gives you no exemption from other obligations.

Take care, my son, to be in reality what others promise or pretend to be: you have patterns set you in your own family; patterns that represent to you human virtues in an eminent degree. You have them all before you in your father. I shall say nothing of his talents for war; it does not become me to speak of them; but the use the king made of them, and the various posts of trust that he gave him, are sufficient proofs that he deserved his confidence.

The king often said that he was one of his best officers, on whom he depended most. This was but part of his merit, for he had all the social virtues: he knew how to reconcile ambition with moderation; he aspired to true glory, without troubling himself about making his fortune; he was neglected for a considerable time, and met with a sort

G

of injustice. In that unlucky season, when your
father was under the frowns of fortune, (a juncture
when any body but he would have been tired out,)
with what courage did he bear his ill treatment ?
He resolved, by failing in no part of his duty, to
bring fortune over to his side, or leave her inexcu-
sable : his notion was, that true ambition consisted
rather in making ones-self superior in merit than in
dignity.

There are some virtues that are not to be acquired but in disgrace : we know not what we are till
we have been tried.   The virtues of prosperity are
pleasant and easy ; those of adversity are harsh
and difficult, and require all the powers of a man
to enable him to practise them.   He knew how to
suffer without desponding, for he had an infinite
number of resources in himself; he thought he was
obliged in duty to continue in his profession, being
convinced, that the slowness of recompenses never
authorizes us to quit the service.   His misfortunes
never shook his courage in the least; he knew how
to bear them with patience and dignity, and how to
enjoy prosperity without haughtiness and pride.—
The change of fortune made none at all in his mind,
and did not cost him a single virtue.

When he was made governor of Luxemburg, all
the province was in dread of the French dominion :
he cured the people entirely of their fears; so that
they were scarcely sensible they had changed masters. He had a light hand, and governed only by
love, and never by authority ; he made nobody feel
the distance between him and others.   His goodness cut short the way that divided him from his
inferiors; he either raised them up to himself, or
else stooped down to them.   He never employed

his credit but to do good. He could not bear to see any body unhappy where he commanded ; all his care was to solicit and get pensions for the officers, and gratifications for the wounded, and such as had distinguished themselves. He made the fortune of abundance of persons.

Self-love got but little by your father's advancement, which was the good of others. This made him the delight of all that lived under his government ; and when he died, if they could have done it, they would have purchased him again with their blood. His good qualities struck envy dumb, and all the world in their hearts applauded the king's disposal of his graces. In an age of general corruption, he had the purest morals; he thought in a different manner from the generality of mankind.

What faithfulness to his word! He always kept it, though at his own expense. What disinterestedness in his conduct ! He never minded his advantage in the least. What allowance did he make for human frailties! He was always excusing the faults of others, and considering them barely as their misfortunes; so that one would be tempted to imagine, that he thought himself the only person in the world that was obliged to be an honest man. His virtues, far from being troublesome to others, left every body at their ease. He had all that amiable complaisance and good nature which is so useful in life, and so necessary for the good correspondence and harmony of mankind. None of his virtues were precarious, because they were all natural. An acquired merit is often uncertain ; but your father, still following reason as his guide, and practising virtue without violence to his nature, never varied at all in his conduct.

See, my son, what we have lost. Such an extraordinary degree of merit seemed to insure us a vast fortune: nothing was more reasonable than our hopes in the reign of so just a prince. Your father, however, left you nothing but his name and example. His name obliges you to bear it with dignity, and his virtues challenge your imitation; it is a model by which you may form yourself: I do not ask more of you, but I will not excuse you for less.

You have this advantage over your ancestors, that they may serve to guide you: I am not ashamed to say, that they left you no fortune; nor would they blush to own it, after employing their estates in the service of their prince, and passing through life without any injustice to others, or any meanness in their own conduct.

Great fortunes are so seldom innocent, that I easily forgive your ancestors for not leaving you any. I have done all I could to bring our affairs into some order; a point in which women can distinguish themselves no way but by economy. I shall do my utmost to discharge every duty incumbent upon me in my circumstances: I shall leave you as much as is fitting for you, if you are so unhappy as to have no merit; and enough, in all reason, if you have the virtues I wish you.

As I desire nothing upon earth so much as to see you a perfectly honest man, let us see what sort of conduct is necessary to give one a title to that character, that we may know what we ought to do to deserve it. I improve myself by these reflections; and may, perhaps, be one day happy enough to change my precepts into examples.

She that exhorts another ought to lead the way

herself. A Persian ambassador asked the wife of
Leonidas, 'Why they paid such honors to the women at Lacedæmon?' 'It is,' replied she, 'because
they have entirely the forming of the men.' A
Greek lady showed her jewels to Phocion's mother,
and asked to see hers: the noble Athenian pointed
to her children, and said to her, ' These are my finery and jewels.' I hope my son, to find in time a
like subject of glory in you.—But let us return to the
obligations which men are obliged to discharge.

There is a certain order in these obligations. A
man should know how to live with his superiors, his
equals, and his inferiors, as well as with himself.
With his superiors, he should know how to please
without sinking into meanness, should show an esteem and friendship to his equals, should conde-
scend to his inferiors so as not to let them feel the
weight of his superiority, and should keep up a
dignity with himself.

All these obligations are still inferior to the veneration you owe to the Supreme Being. Religion
is a correspondence settled between God and man,
by the favours of God to men, and the worship that
men pay to God. Souls of a superior genius have
noble sentiments for the Deity, and pay him a worship peculiar to themselves, very different from that
of the vulgar; it all comes from their heart, and
is directed immediately to God. Moral virtues are
very precarious, without the Christian to support
them. I do not recommend to you a piety blend-
ed with weakness and superstition: I only insist,
that the love of order should make you submit
your understanding and sentiments to God, and
should show itself in every part of your conduct; it
will inspire justice into you, and justice is the basis
of all other virtues.

The generality of young men think to distinguish themselves now-a-days by assuming a libertine air, which degrades them among men of sense; such an air, instead of arguing a superiority of understanding, shows only the depravity of the heart. People never attack religion, but when they have an interest to attack it: nothing makes a man happier than to have his understanding convinced, and his heart affected with it: it is of excellent use in every season and circumstance of life. Such as are not happy enough to believe as they ought, do yet find it reasonable to submit to the established religion: they know that what is miscalled prejudice has a great vogue in the world, and ought to be treated with respect.

A libertine way of thinking, and licentiousness of manners, ought to be banished under the present reign.

The behaviour of the soverelgn is a sort of law to regulate that of others; it enjoins whatever he practises, and forbids what he declines doing. The failings of princes are multiplied, and their virtues are renewed, by imitation. Though courtiers should be debauched in their sentiments, there is still a politeness reigning at court, which serves to throw a veil over vice. We have the good fortune to be born in an age when purity of morals and a respect for religion are necessary to please the prince.

I might, my son, in the order of your duties, insist on what you owe to me; but I would derive it entirely from your heart. Consider the condition in which your father left me: I had sacrificed all that belonged to me to raise his fortune, and I lost my all at his death. I saw myself left alone, des-

tiaute of any support. I had no friends but his;
and I found by experience, that few persons are capable of being friends to the dead. I met with enemies in my own family: I had a law-suit upon my
hands against potent adversaries, and my whole
fortune depended on the event. I gained it at
last without any power of my own, and without
any cringing to others. In a word, I made the
best I could of my ill circumstances; and as soon
as ever my own fortune was mended, I set myself
to make yours. Give me the same share in your
friendship that I shall give you in my little fortune.

I will have no affected respect: I would have all
your regards to me come not from constraint, but
purely from your heart. Let them proceed entirely
from your inclinations, without being influenced by
any motive of interest. In short, take care of your
own glory, and I will take care of every thing else.

You know how to conduct yourself with your
superiors: but there are still some instructions to
be given with regard to the duty you owe your
prince. You are of a family that has sacrificed
their all for him. As for the persons on whom you
depend—the first merit is to please.

In subaltern employments you have no way to
support yourself but by being agreeable: masters
are just like mistresses; whatever service you have
done them, they cease to love you as soon as you
cease to please them.

There are various sorts of dignity, and they require as various kinds of respect.

There are real and personal dignities, and there
are dignities of institution: there is always a respect
due to persons in elevated stations, but it is merely

an outward respect . our real respect and esteem
are due only to merit. When fortune and virtue
have concurred to raise a man to a high post, there
is a double empire in the case, which commands a
double submission : but let not the glittering of
grandeur dazzle and impose upon you.

There are some mean souls that are always
crouching and grovelling before grandeur. One
ought to separate the man from the dignity, and see
what he is when he is stripped of it. There is
another greatness very different from that which
power and authority give. It is neither birth nor
riches that distinguishes men : the only real and
true superiority among them is merit.

The character of an honest man is a nobler title
than any that fortune can bestow. In subaltern
posts one is necessarily dependant : one must make
one's court to the ministers ; but it must be made
with dignity. I shall never give you any cringing
lectures : it is your services that should speak for
you, and not any unbecoming submissions.

Men of merit, when they make their court to ministers, do them an honour, but scoundrels disgrace
them. Nothing is more agreeable than to be a
friend of persons of dignity ; but what lays the
foundation of this friendship is a desire to please
them.

Let your acquaintance be with persons that are
above you : you will by that means get a habit of
respect and politeness. People are too careless
when they converse with their equals : they grow
dull, for want of exerting their parts.

I do not know whether one may hope to find
friends at court. As for persons of eminent dignity,
their post exempts them from   great many duties,

and covers abundance of their failings. It is good
to examine into men to know them thoroughly, and
see them with their every day's merit about them.
The favourites of fortune impose upon you, when
you look upon them at a distance: the distance
puts them in a point of view that is favourable to
them; Fame always enhances their merit, and
Flattery defies them. Examine them near, and
you will find them to be but men. What a number
of ordinary creatures do we find at court! to rectify one's notions of greatness, one must view it
near; you will cease immediately either to desire
or fear it.

Let not the failings of great men corrupt you,
but rather teach you to correct your own. Let the
ill use which they make of their estates teach you
to despise riches, and keep yourself within bounds.
Virtue seldom has the direction of their expenses.

Among the infinite number of tastes invented by
luxury and sensuality, why has there not been one
formed for relieving the miserable? Does not humanity itself make you feel the necessity of assist-
ing your fellow-creatures? Good-natured and generous tempers are more sensible of the obligation
that lies upon them to do good, than they are of
all the other necessities of life. Marcus Aurelius
thanked the gods for his having always done good
to his friends, without making them wait for it. It
is the great felicity of grandeur, when others find
their fortune in ours. 'I cannot,' said that prince,
'have any relish of a happiness that nobody shares
in but myself.'

The most exquisite pleasure in nature is to make
the pleasure of others: but for this end one must
not be too fond of the goods of fortune. Riches

never were the parent of virtue, but virtue has often been the cause of riches. What use, too, do the generality of great men make of the glory of their station? They put it all in exterior marks, and in an air of pride : their dignity sits heavy on them, and depresses others ; whereas true greatness is humane ; it is always easy of access, and condescends even to stoop to you ; such as really enjoy it are at their ease, and make others so too as well as themselves. Their advancement does not cost them any virtue, and the nobleness of their sentiments had formed, and in a manner habituated them to it before-hand. Their elevated station seems natural to them, and nobody is a sufferer by it.

Titles and dignities are not the bonds that unite us to men, or gain them to us : without merit and beneficence to recommend our grandeur to them, we have but a precarious tenure of their friendship , and they will only seek to indemnify themselves at our expense for the homage which they have been forced to pay to the post, rather than to the man that enjoys it, whom they will not fail to arraign freely, and condemn in his absence. If envy be the motive that makes us love to lessen the good qualities of men, in great posts, it is a passion we ought to oppose, and render them the justice that they deserve. We fancy frequently that we have no grudge but against the men, when indeed our malignity is owing to their places : persons in great posts never yet enjoyed them with the good liking of the world, which only begins to do them justice when they are out of place. Envy, in spite of itself, pays a homage to greatness at the same time that it seems to despise it ; for to envy places is to honour them. Let us not out of discontent condemn agreeable stations, which have no fault but that we are not in them ourselves.—It is time now to pass to the duties of society.

Men have found it necessary as well as agreeable to unite for the common good : they have made laws to restrain the wicked ; they have agreed amongst themselves as to the duties of society, and have annexed an honourable character to the practice of those duties. He is the honest man that observes them with the most exactness, and the instances of them multiply in proportion to the degree and nicety of a persons honour.

Virtues are linked together, and have a sort of alliance with one another : what constitutes a hero is the union of all the virtues. After prescribing the duties necessary for their common security, men set themselves to make their conversation agreeable, and settle certain rules of politeness and living to be observed by persons of birth and quality.

There are some failings against which no precepts are to be given : there are certain vices that are unknown to men of honour. Probity, fidelity in keeping one's word, and a love of truth, are subjects that I think I need not insist on and recommend to you: you know that a man of honour knows not what it is to tell a lie. What eulogiums does not the world give, and give deservedly, to lovers of truth. The man, say they, that does good aud speaks the truth, resembles the Deity, whose essential properties are goodness and truth. We aro not indeed obliged always to speak what we think, but we must always think what we speak. The true use of speech is to promote truth. When a man has acquired a reputation for veracity, his word is taken implicitly: it has all the authority of an oath, and the world receives what he says with a sort of religious respect

Falsehood in actions is full as inconsistent with a love of truth as falsehood in words. Men of honour are never false; what, indeed, have they to disguise? Nor are they fond of showing themselves; because, sooner or later, true merit will make its way.

Remember that the world will sooner pardon you your failings, than the affectation of pretending to virtues which you have not in reality. Falsehood affects to put on the air of truth, but a false man's professions go no farther than his looks and discourses; whereas a man's of veracity are made good by his actions. It has been said a long time ago, that hypocrisy is a homage which vice pays to virtue : but the principal virtues are not of themselves sufficient to qualify a man to please : he must have, likewise, agreeable and engaging qualities.

When one aims at gaining a great reputation, one is always in a state of dependence on the opinion of others. It is very difficult for a man to rise to honours by his services, unless he has friends to set them forth, and a manner of behaviour proper to recommend them.

I have told you already, that in subaltern posts a man cannot support himself but by a knack of pleasing; as soon as ever he is neglected, he becomes from that moment inconsiderable. There is nothing so disagreeable as to show a too great fondness for one's self, and expose one's vanity, so as to make people see that we like ourselves above all the world, and that every thing centres in us.

A man with a great deal of wit may make himself very agreeable, when he only employs it to find out the failings of others, and expose them publicly. As for this sort of men, who only show their wit at other people's expense, they ought to consider that nobody's life is so perfectly without a blemish, as to give him a right to censure another man's.

Raillery makes a part of the amusements of conversation, but is a very nice matter to manage. Persons that want to traduce, and love to rally, have a secret malignity in their heart. The most agreeable raillery in nature gives offence, if it advances a step too far; so easy is the transition from the one to the other. A false friend often abuses the liberty of banter, and reflects upon you. In all cases of this nature, the person that you attack has the sole right of judging whether you are in jest or not; the moment he takes offence, it ceases to be raillery; it is a downright affront.

Raillery should never be used but with regard to failings of so little consequence, that the person concerned may be merry on the subject himself. Nice raillery is a decent mixture of praise and reproach; it touches slightly upon little failings, only to dwell the more upon great qualities. Monsier de la Rochefoucault says, that 'the man who dishonours another, does less mischief than he that ridicules him.' I should be of his opinion for this reason, that it is not in any body's power to dishonour another: it is not the discourse or reflection of others, it is only our own conduct that can dishonour us. The causes of dishonour are known and certain, but ridicule is entirely arbitrary; it depends on the manner how objects appear to us, and on

our manner of thinking and taking them. There
are some people that may be said to wear always
spectacles of ridicule, and see every thing through
them. It is not so much the fault of objects, as the
fault of persons that view them in such a light:
this is so true, that such persons as appear ridiculous, in certain companies, would be admired in
others where there are men of sense and merit.

A man's humour, too, contributes much to the
making him agreeable or otherwise: dark and sour
humours, that have a spice of malevolence in them,
are vastly disagreeable.

Humour is the disposition with which the soul receives the impression of objects: good-natured tempers take nothing ill; their indulgence is of benefit
to others, and supplies them with what they want in
themselves.

The generality of mankind imagine that it is to
no purpose to attempt to correct their humour; they
say, 'I was born so;' and fancy this is excuse
enough to justify their not taking any pains about
it. Such tempers must infallibly displease: men
owe you nothing, any farther than you are agreeable to them. The way to be so is to forget one's
self; to put others upon subjects that they like; to
make them pleased with themselves; to set them
out with advantage, and allow them the good qualities which others dispute their having. They believe you give them what the world does not allow
them; their merit seems, in some sort, to be of your
creation, whilst you exalt them in the opinion of
others: but this is never to be pushed so far as to
commence flattery.

Nothing pleases so much as sensible and tender
persons trying to make a friendship with others.

Take care to carry yourself in such a manner, that your behaviour may at once make a tender of your own friendship, and invite the friendship of others: You can never be an amiable man without knowing how to be a friend, without a taste and knowledge of friendship. It is this corrects the vices of society; it softens the roughness of people's natures; it brings down their vanity, and makes them know themselves. All the obligations of honour are included in the obligations of perfect friendship.

In the hurry and bustle of the world, take care, my son, to have a sure friend to whisper truth to your soul: be always ready to hear the advice of your friends. The owning of faults is no hard matter for persons that find a fund within themselves to mend them: think that you have never done enough, when you find that you can still do better. Nobody takes a reproof so kindly as he that deserves most to be commended. If you are happy enough to find a true friend, you have found a treasure: his reputation will secure your own; he will answer for you to yourself; he will alleviate all your troubles, and multiply all your pleasures. But if you would deserve a friend, you must know how to be one.

All the world is complaining of the want of friends, and yet scarcely any body gives himself the trouble of bringing the necessary dispositions to gain and preserve them. Young men have their companions, but they very rarely have any friends: pleasures are what unite them, but pleasures are not ties worthy of friendship. I do not pretend to make a dissertation on this subject; I only touch slightly on some duties of civil life; I refer you to your own heart, which will put you upon desiring a friend, and make you feel the necessity of having one. I depend upon the niceness of your sentiments to instruct you in the duties of friendship.

If you would be perfectly an honest man, you must think of keeping your self-love within bounds, and placing it on a good object. Honesty consists in waving one's own rights, and paying a regard to those of others. If you set up to be happy alone, you will never be so; all the world will dispute your happiness with you: but if you are for making the world happy as well as yourself, every body will assist you. All vices whatever flatter self-love, and all the virtues agree to attack it; valour exposes it; modesty lowers it; generosity throws it away; moderation mortifies it; and zeal for the public sacrifices it to the good of society.

Self-love is a preferring of one's self to others, as honesty is the preferring of others to one's self. There are two kinds of self-love; the one natural, lawful, and regulated by justice and reason; the other vicious and corrupt. Our first object is certainly ourselves; it is only reflection that calls us back to justice. We do not know how to love ourselves; we either carry our self-love too high, or exercise it improperly. To love one's self as one ought, is to love virtue; to love vice is to strike in with a blind and mistaken love.

We have sometimes seen persons advance themselves by ill ways; but if vice is preferred, it is not for any length of time; corrupt persons ruin themselves by the very means, and with the same principles, that raised them. If you would be happy with security, you must be so with innocence. There is no power sure and lasting, but that of virtue.

There are some amiable tempers that have a fine and natural congruity with virtue: those to whom nature has not been so bountiful, must be watchful over their conduct, and know their true interest, to be able to correct an evil disposition. Thus the understanding rectifies the heart.

The love of esteem is the life and soul of society; it unites us to one another: I want your approbation, you stand in need of mine. By forsaking the converse of men, we forsake the virtues necessary for society; for when one is alone, one is apt to grow negligent; the world forces you to have a guard over yourself.

Politeness is the most necessary quality for conversation; it is the art of employing the exterior marks of breeding, which, after all, gives us no assurance of a man's inward qualities. Politeness is an imitation of honesty, and shows a man in his outside, such as he ought to be within; it discovers itself in every thing, in his air, in his discourse, and in his actions.

There is a politeness of understanding, and a politeness of manners: that of the understanding consists in saying curious and ingenious things · that of manners, in saying things of a flattering nature and an agreeable turn.

I do not confine politeness to that intercourse of civilities and compliments, which is settled by common use; they are made without meaning, and received without any sense of obligation; people are apt to over-do the matter in this sort of intercourse, and abate of it upon experience

Politeness is a desire to please the persons with whom we are obliged to live, and to behave ourselves in such a manner, that all the world may be

satisfied with us: our superiors with our respect;
our equals with our esteem; and our inferiors with
our kindness and condescension. In a word, it
consists in a care to please, and say what is proper
to every body. It sets out their good qualities; it
makes them sensible that you acknowledge their
superiority: when you know how to exalt them,
they will set you out in their turn; they will give
you the same preference to others, which you are
pleased to give them to yourself: their self-love obliges them to do so.

The way to please is not to display your superiority; it is to conceal it from being perceived.
There is a great deal of judgment in being polite;
but the world will excuse you at an easier rate.

The generality of people require only certain
manners that please: if you have them not, you
must make up the defect with the number of your
good qualities. There must be a great deal of
merit to get over a clownish awkward behaviour.
Never let the world see that you are fond of your
own person: a polite man never finds time to talk
of himself.

You know what sort of politeness is necessary to
be observed to the women. At present it looks as
if the young men had made a vow not to practise
it; it is a sign of a careless education.

Nothing is more shameful than a voluntary rudeness; but, let them do their worst, they can never
rob the women of the glory of having formed the
finest gentlemen of the last age. It is to them that
they owed all the complaisance of behaviour, the
delicacy of inclinations, and the fine gallantry of
wit and manners which were then remarkable

At present, indeed, exterior gallantry seems to

be banished; the manners of the world are different, and every body has lost something by the
change; the women the desire of pleasing, which
was the source of their charms; and the men the
complaisance and fine politeness, which is only to
be acquired in their conversation. The generality
of men fancy that they owe them neither probity
nor fidelity: it looks as if they had a license to betray them, without affecting their honour. Who
ever would think fit to examine into the motives of
such a conduct, would find them very scandalous.
They are faithful to one another, because they are
afraid, and know they shall be called to an account; but they are false to the women without
fear of suffering and without remorse. This shews
their probity to be only forced, to be rather the effect of fear than the love of justice; and, accordingly, if we examine close into such as make a
trade of gallantry, we shall find them frequently to
be men of no honour; they contract ill-habits; their
manners are corrupted; they grow indifferent to
truth, and indulge themselves in their habitual neglect of their word and oaths. What a trade is
this! where the least ill thing that you do is to seduce the women from their duty, to dishonour
some, to make others desperate, where a sure cala-
mity is oftentimes all the recompense of a sincere
and constant affection.

The men have no reason to find so much fault
with the women; for it is by them that they lose
their innocence. If we except some women, that
seem destined to vice from their cradle, the rest
would live in a regular practice of their duty, if the
men did not take pains to turn them from it: but,
in short, it is their business to be on their guard

against them. You know that it is never allow
able to dishonour them: if they have had the
weakness to trust you with their honour, it is a
confidence that you ought not to abuse. You owe
it to them, if you have reason to be satisfied with
them ; you owe it to yourself, if you have reason
to complain of them. You know, too, that by the
laws of honour you must fight with equal weap-
ons ; you ought not therefore to expose a woman
to dishonour for her amour, since she can never
expose you for yours.

I must, however, caution you against incurring
their hatred; it is violent and implacable: there
are some offences which they never pardon, and
people run a greater risk than they imagine in
wounding their honour; the less their resentment
breaks out, the more terrible is it ; by being held
in, it grows the fiercer. Have no quarrel with a
sex that knows so well how to resent and revenge
themselves; and the rather, because the women
make the reputation of the men, as the men make
that of the women.

It is a happy talent, but very rarely to be met
with, to know how to manage the point of praise,
to give it agreeably and with justice. The morose
man does not know how to praise ; his judgment is
spoiled by his temper. The flatterer, by praising
too much, ruins his own credit, and does honour to
nobody. The vain man deals out his praises only
to receive others in return ; he shows too plainly
that he praises merely out of affectation. Shallow
understandings esteem every thing, because they
know not the value of things: they cannot make
either their esteem or contempt pass in the world.
The envious wretch praises nobody, for fear of put-

ting others on a level with himself. An honest man praises in the right place; he feels more pleasure in doing justice than in raising his own reputation by lessening that of others. Persons that reflect, and are nice upon this article, are very sensible of all these differences. If you would have your praises of any body be of service to you, always praise out of regard you have for others, and not out of any regard to yourself.

One should know how to live with one's competitors: there is nothing more common than to wish to raise one's self above them, or try to ruin them: but there is a much nobler conduct; it is never to attack them, and always strive to exceed them in merit; it is a handsome action to yield them the place which you think is due to them.

An honest man chooses rather to neglect his own fortune, than to fail in a point of justice. Dispute about glory with yourself, and strive to acquire new virtues, and to improve the merit of those which you have already.

One must be very cautious in the article of revenge; it is often of use to make one's self feared; but it is almost always dangerous to revenge one's self. There is not a greater weakness than to do all the mischief that we can. The best manner of revenging an injury, is not to imitate the person that did it. It is a fight worthy of honest men, to oppose patience to passion, and moderation to injustice. An extravagant hatred puts you beneath the persons that you hate. Do not justify your enemies; do nothing that can excuse them: they do us less mischief than our own faults. Little souls are cruel, but clemency is the virtue of great men. Cæsar said, that ' the most agreeable fruit of his

victories, was the having it in his power to give
people their lives who attempted his own.' There
is nothing more glorious and exquisite than this
kind of revenge; it is the only one that men of
honour allow themselves to take. As soon as your
enemy repents and makes his submission, you lose
all manner of right to revenge.

The generality of mankind bring nothing into the
intercourse of life but their weakness, which serves
for society. Honest men form an intimacy by their
virtues, the ordinary sort of men by their pleasures,
and villains by their crimes.

Good-fellowship and gaming have their excess
and their dangers: love has others peculiar to itself:
there is no playing always with beauty; it sometimes commands imperiously. There is nothing
more shameful in a man than excessive drinking,
and drowning his reason, which ought to be the
guide of his life. To give one's self to voluptuousness is to degrade one's nature. The surest way to
avoid it, is not to grow familiar with it: one would
think the voluptuous man's soul was a charge to him.

As for gaming, it is the destruction of all decorum. The prince forgets his dignity at it, and the
woman her modesty. Deep play carries with it
all the social vices. They rendezvous at certain
hours to hate and ruin one another: it is a great
trial of probity; and few people have preserved
theirs unspotted in a course of gaming.

The most necessary disposition to relish pleasures
is to know how to be without them. Sensual pleasure is out of the way of reasonable persons. Let
your pleasures be ever so great, remember still to
expect some melancholy affair to disturb them, or
some vexatious one to end them.

Wisdom makes use of the love of glory to guard against the meanness into which sensuality hurries a man. But one must set to work betimes to keep one's self free from passions; they may in the beginning be under command, but they domineer at last: they are more easy to be overcome than satisfied.

Keep yourself from envy; it is the lowest and most shameful passion in the world; it is always disowned. Envy is the shadow of glory, as glory is the shadow of virtue. The greatest sign that a man is born with great qualities is to say, that he has no envy in his nature.

A man of quality can never be amiable without liberality. The covetous man cannot fail of being disagreeable. He has within him an obstacle to all virtues: he has neither justice nor humanity. When once a man gives up himself to avarice, he renounces glory: it is said, there have been illustrious villains, but that there never were any illustrious misers.

Though liberality is a gift of nature, yet, if we had a disposition to the contrary vice, we might by good sense and reflection correct it.

The covetous man enjoys nothing. Money has been said to be a good servant, though an ill master; but it is good on account of the use we can make of it.

The covetous wretch is more tormented than the poor man. The love of riches is the root of all vices, as disinterestedness is the first principle of all virtues.

Riches must be immense in order to be entitled to the first place among the goods of life: they are indeed the first object of the desires of the greatest

part of mankind; yet virtue, glory, and a great reputation, are vastly preferable to all the gifts of
fortune.

The most sensible pleasure of honest men is to
do good and relieve the miserable. What a wide
difference is there between having a little more
money or losing it for one's diversion, and the parting
with it in exchange for the reputation of goodness
and generosity! It is a sacrifice that you make to
your glory. Deny yourself something, to lay up a
fund for your liberality; it is an excellent point of
economy, which naturally tends to advance you
and gain you a good character.

A great reputation is a good treasure. We must
not imagine that a great fortune is necessary to enable one to do good; all the world can do it in
their several stations, with a little attention to themselves and others: fix this inclination in your
heart, and you will find wherewith to gratify it:
occasions enough offer themselves before you, and
there are but too many unhappy persons that solicit you.

Liberality distinguishes itself in the manner of
giving. The liberal man doubles the merit of a
present by the good will with which he makes it:
the covetous wretch spoils it by his regret at parting with it. Liberality never ruined any body.
Families are not raised by avarice, but they are
supported by justice, moderation, and integrity.
Liberality is one of the duties of a noble birth.
When you do good, you only pay a debt; but still
prudence is to govern you in such cases: the principles of profuseness are not shameful, but the consequences of it are dangerous.

There are few men know how to live with their

inferiors. The great opinion that we entertain of ourselves makes us look upon all below us as a distinct species; but how contrary are such sentiments to humanity! If you would raise yourself a great name, you must be affable and easy of access: your military profession gives you no dispensation in this point. Germanicus was adored by his soldiers. To learn what they thought of him, he walked one evening through his camp, and overheard what they said at their little meals, where they take upon them to pass their judgment on their general : 'He went,' says Tacitus, 'to enjoy his reputation and glory.'

You must command by example, rather than authority. Admiration forces men to imitation much sooner than command. To live at your ease, and treat your soldiers harshly, is to be their tyrant, and not their general.

Consider with what view authority was first instituted, and in what manner it should be exercised: it is virtue, and the natural respect which the world pays to it, that made men consent to obedience. You are an usurper of authority, if you do not possess it upon that footing. In an empire where reason shall govern, all the world should be on a level, and no distinction be paid but to virtue.

Humanity itself suffers by the vast difference that fortune has put between one man and another. It is not any dignity or haughtiness, but your merit, that should distinguish you from the vulgar. Consider the advantages of a noble birth and high station only as goods which fortune lends you, and not as distinctions annexed to your person, and that make a part of yourself. If your quality raises you above the ordinary world, think how much you

H

have in common with other men by your weaknesses, which confound you with them : let justice, then, stop the motions of your pride, which would distinguish you from them.

Know, that the first laws which you ought to obey, are those of humanity : remember that you are a man, and that you command over men. When the son of Marcus Aurelius lost his preceptor, the courtiers found fault with him for weeping on that occasion. Marcus Aurelius said to them, ' Allow my son to be a man before he comes to be an emperor.'

Forget always what you are, when humanity requires it of you ; but never forget it when true glory calls upon you to remember it. In fine, if you have any authority, use it only for the happiness of others. Admit them near you, if you are great yourself, instead of keeping them at a distance : never make them feel their inferiority ; and live with them as you would have your superiors live with you.

The greatest part of mankind do not know how to live with themselves : all their care is rather how to get rid of themselves, and they spend their time in seeking for happiness in exterior objects. You should, if it be possible, fix your felicity within yourself, and find in your own breast an equivalent for the advantages which fortune denies you : you will be more easy as to them ; but it must be a principle of reason that brings you thus to yourself, and not an aversion for mankind.

You love solitude ; they reproach you with being too private ; I do not find fault with your taste, but you must not let the social virtues suffer from it. Retire into yourself says Marcus Aurelius ; practiss often this retreat of the soul, you will improve yourself by it. Have some maxim to call up your reason, and fortify your principles upon occasion. Your retirement makes you acquainted with good authors; judicious men do not crowd their minds indifferently with all sorts of learning, but choose their subject.

Take care that your studies influence your manners, and that all the profit of your reading be turned to virtue. Try to find out the first principles of things, and do not subject yourself servilely to the opinions of the vulgar.

Your ordinary reading should be history, but always use reflection with it. If you only think of filling your memory with facts, and polishing your mind with the thoughts and opinions of the ancients, you will only lay up a magazine of other people's notions; one quarter of an hour's reflection improves and forms the mind more than a great deal of reading. A want of learning is not so much to be dreaded, as error and false judgments.

Reflection is the guide that leads to truth: consider facts only as authorities to support reason, or as subjects to exercise it.

History will instruct you in your business; but after you have drawn from it all the advantage proper for your profession, there is a moral use to be made of it, which is of much greater consequence to you.

The first science of man is human nature. Leave politics to ministers, and what belongs to grandeur to princes; but do you find out the man in the prince ; observe him in the course of common life ; see how low he sinks, when he gives himself up to his passions. An irregular conduct is always followed with dismal consequences.

To study history, is to study the passions and opinions of men; it is to examine them thoroughly; it is to pull the mask off their actions, which appeared great whilst they were veiled, and consecrated by success, but often become contemptible when the motive of them is known. There is nothing more ambiguous than the actions of men. We must trace them up to their principles, if we would know them rightly. It is necessary to be sure of the spirit of our actions, before we glory in them.

We do little good, and a great deal of ill; and have the knack, too, of spoiling and depraving the little good that we do.

See princes in history, and elsewhere, as so many actors on the stage; they no way concern you, but by the qualities which we have in common with them. This is so true, that such historians as have set themselves to describe them rather as men than kings, and show them to us in their private life, give us the most pleasure; we find ourselves out in them; we love to see our own weaknesses in great men. This consoles us, in some measure, for our own lowness, and raises us, in some sort, to their elevation. In short, consider a history as a register of times and a picture of manners: you may discover yourself there, without any offence to your vanity.

I shall exhort you, my son, rather to take pains with your heart, than to improve your understanding: that ought to be the great study of your life. The true greatness of man lies in the heart; it must be elevated by aspiring to great things, and by daring to think ourselves worthy of them. It is as becoming to encourage a little vanity within one's self, as it is ridiculous to show it to others.

Take care to have thoughts and sentiments worthy of you. Virtue raises the dignity of man, and vice degrades him. If one was unhappy enough to want an honest heart, one ought for one's own interest to correct it; nothing makes a man truly valuable but his heart, and nothing but that can make him happy; since our happiness depends only on the nature of our inclinations. If they are such as lead you to trifling passions, you will be the sport of their vain attachments; they offer you ' flowers; but always (as Montaigne says) mistrust the treachery of your pleasures.'

We must not indulge ourselves long in things that please us: the moment that we give ourselves up to them, we lay the foundation of our sorrows. The generality of mankind employ the first part of their life in making the rest of it miserable. You must not abandon reason in your pleasures, if you would find it again in your troubles.

In short, keep a strict guard over your heart; it is the source of innocence and happiness. You will not pay too dear for the freedom of your mind and heart, though you purchase it by the sacrifice of your pleasures, as was the saying of an ingenious man. Never expect, then, to reconcile sensuality with glory, or the charm of voluptuousness with the recompense of virtue. However, when you bid adieu to pleasures, you will find in other things satisfaction enough to make you amends. There are various sorts of it; glory and truth have their pleasures; they are the delights of the soul and heart.

Learn likewise to reverence and stand in awe of yourself. The foundation of happiness is laid in the peace of the mind and secret testimony of the

conscience. By the word conscience, I mean the
inward sense of a nice honour, which assures you
that you have nothing to reproach yourself with.
Again, how happy is it to know how to live with one's
self, to renew your acquaintance there with pleasure, and quit yourself for a time with regret! The
world then indeed is less necessary to you: but
take care it does not make you out of humour with
it; one must not entertain an aversion for men;
they will desert you when you desert them: you
have still occasion for them, you are not either of
an age or profession to do without them; but when
one knows how to live with one's self as well as
with the world, they are two pleasures that support one another.

A passion for glory may contribute greatly to
your advancement and happiness; but it may likewise make you unhappy and despicable, if you
know not how to govern it: it is the most active
and lasting of all your inclinations. The love of
glory is the last passion that quits us; but we must
not confound it with vanity. Vanity aims at the
approbation of other people; true glory, at the secret testimony of the conscience. Endeavour to
gratify the passion that you have for glory; make
sure of this inward testimony: your tribunal is seated in your own breast, why then should you seek
it elsewhere? You can always be a judge of your
own worth. Let men dispute your good qualities,
if they please; as they do not know you, you can
easily console yourself. It is not of so much consequence to be thought an honest man, as to be one.
Such as do not mind the approbation of other people, but only aim at deserving it, take the surest
way to obtain both. What affinity is there between

the greatness of man, and the littleness of the things
which make the subject of his glorying ; there is
nothing so ill suited as his dignity, and the vanity
that he derives from an infinite number of trifling
things: a glory so ill grounded shews a great want
of merit. Persons that are truly great are not subject to the infatuations of vain-glory.

One must, if it be possible, my son, be content
with one's condition in the world : there is nothing
more rare and valuable, than to find persons that
are satisfied with it. It is our own fault. There
is no condition of life so bad, but it has one good
side. Every situation has its point of view ; we
should place it in that favourable light, and shall
find, that it is not the fault of our situations, but
purely our own. We have much more reason to
complain of our own temper than of fortune. We
lay all the blame upon events, when all the fault
lies upon our discontent ; the evil is within us, let
us not seek for it any where else. By qualifying ou
temper, we often change our fortune. It is much
easier for us to adjust ourselves to things, than to
adjust things to ourselves. A great application to
find out a remedy frequently irritates the disease,
and the imagination conspires with the pain to increase and fortify it. A dwelling upon misfortures
renews them, by making them present to the mind.
An useless struggling to get out of our circumstances makes us slower in contracting an acquaintance with them, which would make them sit easy
on us. One must always give way to misfortunes,
and have recourse to patience : it is the only way
to alleviate them.

If you would do yourself justice, you will be content with your situation. I dare say, that after the

loss we have suffered, if you had had another mother, you would be still fuller of complaints. Reflect on the advantages of your condition, and you will be less sensible of the difficulties of it. A wise man, in the same circumstances with others, has more advantages, and feels fewer inconveniences, than they.

You may depend upon it, that there is no condition but has its troubles; it is the situation of human life; there is nothing pure and unblended in it. It is to pretend to exempt one's self from the common law of our nature to expect a constant happiness. The very persons, whom you think the happiest, would hardly appear so to you, if you knew the exact situation of their fortune or their heart. Those that are raised the highest are frequently the most unhappy. With great employments and vulgar maxims, one is always restless and uneasy: it is not places, but reason, that removes anxiety from the mind. If you are wise, fortune can neither increase nor diminish your happiness.

Judge by yourself, and not by the opinions of others. Misfortunes and disorders arise from false judgments; false judgments from our passions; and passions from our conversation with mankind. you always come from them more perfect than you were before. To weaken the impressions that they make upon you, and to moderate your desires and inquietudes, consider that time is continually running away with your pains as well as your pleasures; that every moment, young as you are, carries off a part of yourself; that all things are perpetually sinking into the abyss of past time, thence never to return again.

All that you see greatest on earth meets with the

very same treatment as yourself. The honour, the dignities, the precedences settled among men, are mere shows and ceremonies, without any reality; do not imagine that they are qualities inseparable from their being. Thus ought you to consider such as are above you; but take in your view likewise an infinite number of miserable wretches that are below you: the difference between you and them is owing only to chance; but pride, and the great opinion we have of ourselves, make us think that the good condition we are in is no more than our due, and consider every thing that we do not enjoy as a robbery of what should belong to us: you cannot but see plainly that nothing is more unreasonable than such an imagination. Enjoy, my son, the advantages of your circumstances: but suffer patiently the inconveniences that attend them. Consider, that wherever there are men there are unhappy creatures. Enlarge your mind, if possible, so far as to foresee and know all the accidents that can befall you. In a word, remember that a man's happiness depends on his manners and conduct; but the highest felicity is to seek for it in the paths of innocence, and there one never fails to find it.

MAXIMS

AND

MORAL REFLECTIONS,

BY THE

DUKE DE LA ROCHEFOUCAULT.

The desire of appearing to be persons of ability often prevents our being so.

No accidents are so unlucky, but that the prudent may draw some advantage from them : nor are there any so lucky, but what the imprudent may turn to their prejudice.

Great actions, the lustre of which dazzles us, are re-

---

* See Chesterfield's Letters : Letter 225.
† Letter 273.

presented by politicians as the effect of deep design; whereas they are commonly the effects of caprice and passion. Thus the war between Augustus and Antony, supposed to be owing to their ambition to give a master to the world, arose probably from jealousy.

There is nothing of which we are so liberal as of advice.

We may give advice; but we cannot give conduct.

We are never made so ridiculous by the qualities we have, as by those we affect to have.

We had better appear to be what we are, than affect to appear what we are not.

We judge so superficially of things, that common words and actions, spoke and done in an agreeable manner, with some knowledge of what passes in the world, often succeed beyond the greatest ability.

The ambitious deceive themselves in proposing an end to their ambition; for that end, when attained, becomes a means.

When great men suffer themselves to be subdued by the length of their misfortunes, they discover that the strength of their ambition, not of their understanding, was that which supported them. They discover too, that, allowing for a little vanity, heroes are just like other men.

We pass often from love to ambition; but we seldom return from ambition to love.

Those who apply themselves too much to little things, commonly become incapable of great ones.

Few things are impracticable in themselves; and it is for want of application, rather than of means, that men fail of success.

Avarice is more opposite to economy than liberality

Extreme avarice almost always makes mistakes. There is no passion that oftener misses its aim, nor on which the present has so much influence in prejudice of the future.

Avarice often produces contrary effects. There are many people who sacrifice their whole fortunes to dubious and distant expectations; there are others who contemn great future for little present advantages.

We like better to see those on whom we confer benefits, than those from whom we receive them.

Civility is a desire to receive civility, and to be accounted well-bred.

That conduct often seems ridiculous, the secret reasons of which are wise and solid.

A man often imagines he acts, when he is acted upon; and while his mind aims at one thing, his heart insensibly gravitates towards another.

In conversation, confidence has a greater share than wit.

In love, there are two sorts of constancy: one arises from our continually finding in the favourite object fresh motives to love; the other, from our making it a point of honour to be constant.

None but the contemptible are apprehensive of contempt.

One reason why we meet with so few people who are reasonable and agreeable in conversation is, that there is scarcely any body who does not think more of what he has to say, than of answering what is said to him: Even those who have the most address and politeness, think they do enough if they only seem to be attentive; at the same time

their eyes and their minds betray a distraction as
to what is addressed to them, and an impatience
to return to what they themselves were saying:
not reflecting, that to be thus studious of pleasing
themselves, is but a poor way of pleasing or con-
vincing others; and that to hear patiently, and answer precisely, are the great perfections of conver
sation.

We easily forget crimes that are known only to
ourselves.

The greatest of all cunning is, to seem blind to
the snares laid for us: men are never so easily deceived as while they are endeavouring to deceive
others.

Cunning and treachery proceed from want of capacity.

The sure way to be cheated, is to fancy ourselves
more cunning than others.

Few people are well acquainted with death. It
is generally submitted to through stupidity and custom, not resolution. Most men die merely because
they cannot help it.

Death and the sun are not to be looked at steadily.

It is as easy to deceive ourselves without our
perceiving it, as it is difficult to deceive others
without their perceiving it.

Decency is the least of all laws, but the most
strictly observed.

It is much easier to suppress a first desire, than to
satisfy those that follow.

Before we passionately wish for any thing, we
should examine into the happiness of its possessor.

Were we perfectly acquainted with the object,
we should never passionately desire it.

Were we to take as much pains to be what we

ought, as we do to disguise what we *are*, we might appear like ourselves, without being at the trouble of any disguise at all.

We are so used to disguise ourselves to others, that at last we become disguised even to ourselves.

A man who finds not satisfaction in himself seeks for it in vain elsewhere.

Envy is more irreconcilable than hatred.

Envy is destroyed by true friendship, and coquetry by true love.

A great genius will sincerely acknowledge his defects as well as his perfections : it is a weakness not to own the ill as well as the good that is in us.

Had we no faults ourselves, we should take less pleasure in observing those of others.

Flattery is a sort of bad money, to which our vanity gives currency.

We should manage our fortune like our constitution: enjoy it when good, have patience when bad ; and never apply violent remedies but in cases of necessity.

It is more dishonourable to distrust a friend, than to be deceived by him.

We always love those who admire *us ;* but we do not always love those whom *we* admire.

Rare as true love is, it is less so than true friendship.

The greatest effort of friendship is, not the discovery of our faults to a friend, but the endeavouring to make him see his own.

A fool has not stuff enough to make a good man.

Resolute people alone can be truly good natured ; such as commonly seem so are weak, and easily soured.

Good sense should be the test of all rules, both

ancient and modern : whatever is incompatible with good sense is false.

It is more difficult to prevent being governed, than to govern others.

Gravity is a mysterious carriage of the body, invented to cover the defects of the mind.

A good grace is to the body, what good sense is to the mind.

None are either so happy or so unhappy as they imagine.

We take lesspains to *be* happy, than to *appear* so.

Happiness is in the taste, not in the thing ; and we are made happy by possessing what we ourselves love, not what others think lovely.

When our hatred is violent, it sinks us even beneath those we hate.

Every body speaks well of his heart, but no one dares to speak well of his head.

The head is always the dupe of the heart.

The head cannot long act the part of the heart.

One acquired honour is surety for more.

Hope, deceitful as it is, carries us agreeably through life.

Our humour *is* more in fault than our understanding.

The calm or disquiet of our temper depends not so much on affairs of moment, as on the disposition of the trifles that daily occur.

Hypocrisy is the homage that vice pays to virtue.

It is a mistake to imagine, that the violent passions only, such as ambition and love, can triumph over the rest.   Idleness, languid as it is, often masters them all : she indeed influences all our designs and actions, and insensibly consumes and destroys both passions and virtues.

Idleness is more in the mind than in the body.

Only such persons who avoid giving jealousy are deserving of it.

Jealousy is always born with love, but does not always die with it.

Jealousy is nourished by doubt; it either becomes madness, or ceases as soon as we arrive at certainty.

In jealousy there is less love than self-love.

There is a species of love whose excess prevents jealousy.

Philosophy easily triumphs over past and future ills; but *present* ills triumph over philosophy.

The good we have received from a man should make us bear with the ill he does us.

It is less dangerous to do ill to most men, than to do them too much good.

We seldom find people ungrateful so long as we are in a condition to serve them.

Interest speaks all languages, and acts all parts, even that of *disinterestedness* itself.

Intrepidity is an extraordinary strength of soul, that renders it superior to the trouble, disorder, and emotion which the appearance of danger is apt to excite. By this quality heroes maintain their tranquility, and preserve the free use of their reason, in the most surprising and dreadful accidents.

Every one complains of the badness of his memory, but nobody of his judgment.

To know things well, we should know them in detail; and as that is in a manner infinite, our knowledge, therefore, is always superficial and imperfect.

No disguise can long *conceal* love, where it is, nor *feign* it, where it is not.

To judge of love by most of its effects, one would think it more like hatred than kindness.

There is only one sort of love, but there are a thousand different copies of it.

Love, like fire, cannot subsist without continual motion; it ceases to exist, as soon as it ceases to hope or fear.

There are people who would never have been in love, had they never heard talk of it.

To fall in love is much easier than to get rid of it.

Novelty to love is like the bloom to fruit; it gives a lustre, which is easily effaced, but never returns.

It is impossible to love those a second time whom we have really ceased to love.

In love, those who are *first* cured are *best* cured.

All the passions make us commit faults; but love makes us guilty of the most ridiculous ones.

To study men is more necessary than to study books.

The truly honest man is he who valueth not himself on any thing.

He must be a truly honest man who is willing to be always open to the inspection of honest men.

A man of sense may love like a madman, but never like a fool.

Some people are disgusting with great merit; others with great faults very pleasing.

Our merit procures us the esteem of men of sense, and our good fortune that of the public.

The appearance of merit is oftener rewarded by the world than merit itself.

We should not judge of a man's merit by his great qualities, but by the use he makes of them.

Few people know *how* to be old.

Opportunities make us known to ourselves and others.

The passions are the only orators that always succeed. They are, as it were, nature's art of eloquence, fraught with infallible rules. Simplicity, with the aid of the passions, persuades more than the utmost eloquence without it.

So much injustice and self-interest enter into the composition of the passions, that it is very dangerous to obey their dictates; and we ought to be on our guard against them, even when they seem most reasonable.

Absence destroys small passions, and increases great ones; as the wind extinguishes tapers, and kindles fires.

While the heart is still agitated by the remains of a passion, it is more susceptible of a new one, than when entirely at rest.

He who is pleased with nobody, is much more unhappy than he with whom nobody is pleased.

If we were not proud ourselves, we should not complain of the pride of others.

We promise according to our hopes, and perform according to our fears.

Most men, like plants, have secret properties which chance discovers.

Prudence and love are inconsistent; in proportion as the last increases, the other decreases.

Few are so wise as to prefer useful reproof to treacherous praise

There are reproaches that praise, and praises that reproach

Ambition to merit praise fortifies our virtue. Praise bestowed on wit, valour, and beauty, contributes to their augmentation.

It is not enough to have great qualities, we must also have the management of them.

It is with some good qualities as with the senses; they are incomprehensible and inconceivable to such as are deprived of them.

Naturally to be without envy is a certain indication of great qualities.

Quarrels would never last long, if the fault was on one side only.

We never desire ardently what we desire rationally.

Whatever ignominy we may have incurred, it is almost always in our power to re-establish our reputation.

How can we expect that another should keep our secret, when it is more than we can do ourselves.

Self-love is more artful than the most artful of men.

Self-love, well or ill conducted, constitutes virtue and vice.

Human prudence, rightly understood, is circumspect, enlightened self-love.

Notwithstanding all discoveries that have been made in the regions of self-love, there still remains much *terra incognita*.

It is less difficult to feign the sensations we have not, than to conceal those we have.

Affected simplicity is refined imposture.

The health of the soul is as precarious as that of the body ; for when we seem secure from passions, we are no less in danger of their infection, than we are of falling ill when we appear to be well.

There are relapses in the distempers of the soul as well as in those of the body : thus we often mistake for a cure what is no more than an intermission or a change of disease.

The flaws of the soul resemble the wounds of the body; the scar always appears, and they are in danger of breaking open again.

As it is the characteristic of great wits to say much in few words, so small wits seem to have the gift of speaking much, and saying nothing.

The excessive pleasure we find in talking of ourselves ought to make us apprehensive that it gives but little to our auditors.

It is never more difficult to speak well, than when we are ashamed of our silence.

A good taste is the effect of judgment more than understanding.

Titles, instead of exalting, debase those who act not up to them.

Valeur in a private soldier is a hazardous trade, taken up to get a livelihood.

Perfect valour consists in doing without witnesses all we should be capable of doing before the whole world.

No man can answer for his courage who has never been in danger.

If vanity really overturns not the virtues, it certainly makes them totter.

The most violent passions have their intermissions; vanity alone gives us no respite.

The reason why the pangs of shame and jealousy are so sharp, is this:—vanity gives us no assistance in supporting them.

When our vices have left us, we flatter ourselves that we have left them.

Prosperity is a stronger trial of virtue than adversity.

The virtues are lost in interest, as rivers are in the sea.

To the honour of virtue it must be acknowledged, that the greatest misfortunes befal men from their vices.

We despise not all those who have vices; but we despise all those who have no virtues.

There are people, who, like new songs, are in vogue only for a time.

Those are deceived who imagine wit and judgment to be two distinct things. Judgment is only the perfection of wit, which penetrates into the recesses of things, observes all that merits observation, and perceives what seems imperceptible. We must therefore agree, that it is extensive wit which produces all the effects attributed to judgment.

It is a common fault, never to be satisfied with our fortune, nor dissatisfied with our understanding.

Politeness of mind consists in a courteous and delicate conception.

The defects of the mind, like those of the face, grow worse as we grow old.

It is a better employment of the understanding to bear the misfortunes that actually befal us, than to penetrate into those that may.

Those who have but one sort of wit are sure not to please long.

A man of sense finds less difficulty in submitting to a wrong-headed fellow, than in attempting to set him right.

The labours of the body free men from pains of the mind.

This it is that constitutes the happiness of the poor.

Small geniusses are hurt by small events: great geniusses see through and despise them.

Weakness is more opposite to virtue than is vice itself.

Weak people are incapable of sincerity.

If there be a man whose weak side has never been discovered, it is only because we have never accurately looked for it.

We often forgive those who tire us, but cannot forgive those whom we tire.

We have more power than will; and it is only to disculpate us to ourselves, that we often think things impracticable.

Man's chief wisdom consists in knowing his follies.

Wisdom is to the mind what health is to the body.

The common foible of women who have been handsome, is to forget that they are now no longer so.

Of all the violent passions, that which least misbecomes a woman is love.

Youth is continual intoxication. It is the fever of reason.

THE POLITE PHILOSOPHER.

MRTHOD requires, that in my entrance on this work I should explain the nature of that science to which I have given the name of Polite Philosophy. Though I am not very apt to write methodically, yet I think it becomes me on this occasion to show that my title is somewhat *apropos*.

Folks that are skilled in Greek tell us, that Philosophy means no more than the love of wisdom; and I, by the adjunction of Polite, would be understood to mean that sort of wisdom which teaches men to be at peace in themselves, and neither by their words or behaviour to disturb the peace of others.

Academical critics may perhaps expect that I should at least quote some Greek sage or other, as the patron of that kind of knowledge, which I am about to restore; and as I pique myself on obliging every man in his way, I shall put them in mind of one Aristippus, who was professor of Polite Philosophy at Syracuse, in the days of the famous King Dionysius, in whose favour he stood higher than even Plato himself. Should they go further, and demand an account of his tenets, I must turn them over to Horace, who has comprised them all in one line--

' Omnis Aristippam decuit color, et status, et res.'

Secure, his soul preserv'd a constant frame,
Through every varying scene of life the same.

In the court of the king of Sicily, this wise man enjoyed all the delights that would have satisfied a

sensual mind; but it was the use of these which
shewed him a true philosopher. He was tempo-
rate in them, while he possessed them; and easy
without them, when they were no longer in his
power. In a word, he had the integrity of Diogenes,
without his churlishness; and as his wisdom was
useful to himself, so it rendered him agreeable to
the rest of the world.

Aristippus had many pupils; but for the regular
succession in his school, it has either not been re-
corded by the Greek writers, or at least by any of
them that came to my hand. Among the Romans,
indeed, this kind of knowledge was in the highest
esteem; and that at the time when the reputation
of the commonwealth was at its greatest height.
Scipio was less distinguished by the laurels he had
acquired from foreign conquests, than by the myr-
tle garland he wore as a professor in his art. The
familiar letters of Cicero are so many short lectures
in our science, and the life of Pomponius Atticus, a
praxis on polite philosophy.

I would not be suspected to mention these great
names with an intent to display learning; far be it
from me to write a satire on the age; all I aim at is,
to convince the *beaux esprits* of our times, that what
I teach, they may not receive with disparagement,
since they tread thereby in the same road with the
greatest heroes of antiquity; and in this way at least,
emulate the characters of Alexander and Cæsar.
Or, if those old fashioned commanders excite not
their ambition, I will venture to assure them, that
in this track only they will be able to approach the
immortal Prince Eugene; who, glorious from his
courage, and amiable from his clemency, is yet less
distinguished by his rank than by his politeness.

After naming Prince Eugene, it would debase my subject to add another example. I shall proceed therefore to the taking notice of such qualities of the mind as are requisite for my pupils to have, previous to the receipt of these instructions.

But as vanity is one of the greatest impediments in the road of a polite philosopher; and as he who takes upon himself to be a precepter, ought at least not to give an ill example to his scholars; it will not be improper for me to declare, that, in composing this piece, I had in my eye that precept of Seneca—' Hæc aliis dic, ut dum dicis, audias; ipse scribe, ut dum, scripseris, legas.' Which, for the sake of the ladies, I shall translate into English, and into verse, that I may gratify my own prepensity to rhyming—

> Speaking to others, what you dictate hear;
> And learn yourself, while teaching you appear.

Thus you see me stript of the ill-obeyed authority of a pedagogue ; and are for the future to consider me only as a school-fellow playing the master, that we may the better conquer the difficulties of our task.

To proceed then in the character which, for my own sake as well as yours, I have put on, let me remind you, in the first place,

That Reason, however antique you may think it, is a thing absolutely necessary in the composition of him who endeavours at the acquiring a philosophical politeness; and let us receive it as a maxim, that without Reason there is no being a fine gentleman.

However, to soften, at the same time that we yield to this constraint, I tell my blooming audience

I

with pleasure, that Reason, like a fop's under
waistcoat, may be worn out of sight ; and provided
it be but worn at all, I shall not quarrel with them,
though vivacity, like a laced shirt, be put over it to
conceal it ; for to pursue the comparison, our minds
suffer no less from indiscretion, than our bodies
from the injuries of the weather.

Next to this, another out-of-the-way qualification
must be acquired ; and that is, Calmness. Let not
the smarts of the university, the sparks of the side-
boxes, or the genteel flutterers of the drawing room,
imagine, that I will deprive them of those elevated
enjoyments—drinking tea with a toast, gallanting a
fan, or roving, like a butterfly, through a parterre of
beauties : no ; I am far from being the author of
such severe institutions ; but am, on the contrary,
willing to indulge them in their pleasures, as long
as they preserve their senses. By which l would
be understood to mean, while they act in character,
and suffer not a fond inclination, and aspiring vanity, or a giddy freedom, to transport them into the
doing any thing which may forfeit present advantages, or entail upon them future pain.

I shall have frequent occasions in the following
pages to show from examples, of what mighty use
reason and undisturbed temper are to men of great
commerce in the world ; and therefore shall insist
no further on them here.

The last disposition of the soul which I shall mention, as necessary to him who would become a pro-
ficient in this science, is Good-nature ; a quality
which, as Mr. Dryden said in a dedication to one
of the best-natured men of his time, deserves the
highest esteem, though, from an unaccountable depravity of both taste and morals, it meets with the

lea it. For can there be any thing more amiable in
human nature, than to think, to speak, and to do,
whatever good lies in our power to all? No man
who looks upon the sun, and who feels that cheerfulness which his beams inspire, but would rather
wish himself like so glorious a being, than to resemble the tiger, however formidable for its fierce-
ness; or the serpent, hated for hissing, and dreaded
for his sting. Good-nature may indeed be made
almost diffusive as day-light; but short are the ra-
vages of the tiger, innocent the bite of a serpent, to
the vengeance of a cankered heart, or the malice
of an invenomed tongue. To this let me add another argument in favour of this benevolence of soul;
and farther persuasions will, I flatter myself, be unnecessary. Good-nature adorns every perfection a
man is master of, and throws a veil over every blemish which would otherwise appear. In a word,
like a skilful painter, it places his virtues in the fairest light, and casts all his foibles into shade.

Thus, in a few words, Sense, Moderation, and
Sweetness, are essential to a Polite Philosopher.—
And if you think you cannot acquire these, even lay
my book aside. But before you do that, indulge
me yet a moment longer. Nature denies the first
to few; the second is in every man's power; and
no man need be without the last, who either values
general esteem, or is not indifferent to public hate.
For, to say truth, what is necessary to make an honest man, properly applied, would make a polite
one; and as almost every one would take it amiss,
if we should deny him the first appellation; so you
may perceive from thence how few there are who,
but from their own indiscretion, may deserve the second. It is want of attention, not capacity, which

leaves us so many brutes; and I flatter myself,
there will be fewer of this species, if any of them,
can be prevailed upon to read this. A description
of their faults is to such the fittest lecture; for few
monsters there are who can view themselves in a
glass.

> Our follies, when display'd, ourselves affright
> Few are so bad to bear the odious sight.
> Mankind in herds, thro' force of custom, stray,
> Mislead each other into Error's way,
> Pursue the road, forgetful of the end,
> Sin by mistake, and without thought offend.

My readers, who have been many of them accustomed to think politeness rather an ornamental accomplishment, than a thing necessary to be acquired
in order to an easy and happy life, may from thence
pay less attention than my instructions require, unless I can convince them they are in the wrong. In
order to which, I must put them in mind, that the
tranquillity, even felicity of our days, depends as
strongly on small things as on great; of which men
may be easily convinced, if they but reflect how
great uneasiness they have experienced from cross
accidents, although they related but to trifles; and
at the same time remember that disquiet is of all
others the greatest evil, let it arise from what it will.

Now, in the concerns of life, as in those of fortune, numbers are brought into what are called bad
circumstances from small neglects, rather than from
any great errors in material affairs. People are too
apt to think lightly of shillings and pence, forgetting
that they are the constituent parts of pounds; until
the deficiency in the greater articles shows them
their mistake, and convinces them by fatal experi-

ence of a truth, which they might have learned from
a little attention, viz. that great sums are made up
of small.

Exactly parallel to this, is that wrong notion
which many have, that nothing more is due from
them to their neighbours, than what results from a
principle of honesty,—which commands us to pay
our debts, and forbids to do injuries; whereas a
thousand little civilities, complacencies, and endeavours to give others pleasure, are requisite to
keep up the relish of life, and procure us that affection and esteem, which every man who has a sense
of it must desire. And in the right timing and
discreet management of these punctilios, consists
the essence of what we call politeness.

> How many know the general rules of art,
> Which unto tablets human forms impart ?
> How many can depict the rising brow,
> The nose, the mouth, and every feature shew ?
> Can in their colours imitate the skin,
> And by the force of fire can fix them in ?
> Yet when 'tis done, unpleasing to the sight,
> Tho' like the picture, strikes not with delight.
> 'Tis zinc alone gives the enamel'd face
> A polish'd sweetness and a glossy grace.

Examples have, generally speaking, greater force
than precepts: I will therefore delineate the characters of Honorius and Gracia, two gentlemen of
my acquaintance, whose humour I have perfectly
considered, and shall represent them without the
least exaggeration.

Honorius is a person equally distinguished by
his birth and fortune. He has naturally good sense,
and that too hath been improved by a regular education. His wit is lively, and his morals without a

stain.—Is not this an amiable character ?   Yet Honorius is not beloved.   He has, some way or other,
contracted a notion, that it is beneath a man of honour to fall below the height of truth in any degree,
or on any occasion whatsoever.   From this principle he speaks bluntly what he thinks, without regarding the company who are by.   Some weeks
ago he read a lecture on female hypocrisy before a
married couple, though the lady was much suspected on that head.   Two hours after, he fell into a
warm declamation against simony and priest-craft
before two dignitaries of the church ; and from a
continued course of this sort of behaviour, had rendered himself dreaded as a monitor, instead of being esteemed as a friend.

Gracia, on the contrary, came into the world under the greatest disadvantages.   His birth was
mean, and his fortune not to be mentioned : yet,
though he is scarce forty, he has acquired a handsome fortune in the country, and lives upon it with
more reputation than most of his neighbours.   While
a servitor at the university, he by his assiduities recommended himself to a noble lord, and thereby
procured himself a place of fifty pounds a year in a
public office.   His behaviour there made him as
many friends as there were persons belonging to his
board.   His readiness in doing favours gained him
the hearts of his inferiors ; his deference for those
of the highest characters in the office, procured him
their good will ; and the complacency he expressed
towards his equals, and those immediately above
him, made them espouse his interest with almost as
much warmth as they did their own.   By this management in ten years' time he rose to the possession of an office which brought him in a thousand

pounds a year salary, and nearly double as much
perquisites. Affluence hath made no alteration in
his manners. The same easiness of disposition attends him in that fortune to which it has raised
him,—and he is at this day the delight of all who
know him, from an art he has of persuading them,
that their pleasures and their interests are equally
dear to him with his own. Who, if it were in his
power, would not refuse what Honorius possesses? and who would not wish that possession accompanied with Gracia's disposition?

I flatter myself, that by this time most of my readers have acquired a tolerable idea of politeness,
and a just notion of its use in our passage through
life. I must, however, caution them of one thing,
that under the notion of politeness, they fall neither
into a contempt or carelessness of science.

A man may have much learning without being a
pedant; nay, it is necessary that he should have a
considerable stock of knowledge before he can be
polite. The gloss is never given till the work is finished; without it the best wrought piece is clum-
sy; but varnish over a rough board is a preposterous daub. In a word, that rule of Horace, ' mis-
cere utile dulci,' so often quoted, can never be better applied than in the present case, where neither
of the qualities can subsist without the other.

> With dress, for once, the rule of life we'll place,
> Cloth is plain sense, and polish'd breeding lace.
> Men may in both mistake the true design ;
> Fools oft are tandry, when they would be fine.
> An equal mixture both of use and show,
> From giddy fops points the accomplish'd beau.

Having now gone through the præcognita of Poits Philosophy, it is requisite we should descend with greater particularity into its several branches.

For though exactness would not be a piece either with the nature or intent of this work, yet some order is absolutely necessary, because nothing is more unpolite than to be obscure. Some philosophers have indeed prided themselves in a mysterious way of speaking; wrapping their maxims in so tough a coat, that the kernel, when found, seldom atoned for the pains of the finder.

The polite sage thinks in a quite different way. Perspicuity is the garment in which his conceptions appear; and his sentiments, if they are of any use, carry this additional advantage with them, that scarce any labour is required in attaining them. Graver discourses, like Galenical medicines, are often formidable in their figure, and nauseous in their taste. Lectures from a doctor in our science, like a chemical extraction, convey knowledge, as it were, by drops, and restore sense as the other does the health, without the apparatus of physic.

> Harsh to the heart, and grating to the ear,
> Who can reproof without reluctance hear?
> Why against priests the gen'ral heat so strong,
> But that they show us all we do is wrong?
> Wit well apply'd does weightier wisdom right,
> And gives us knowledge, while it gives delight.
> Thus, on the stage, we with applause behold,
> What would have pain'd us from the pulpit told.

It is now time to apply what we have already advanced to those points in which they may be the most useful to us; and therefore we will begin, by considering what advantage the practice of them will procure in respect to those three things which are esteemed of the greatest consequence in the general opinion of the world. This leads me, in the first place, to explain the sentiments and conduct of a polite philosopher in regard to religion. I am not ignorant, that there are a multitude of those who pass both on the world and on themselves for very polite persons, who look on this as a topic below their notice. Religion (say they with a sneer) is the companion of melancholy minds; but for the gayer part of the world, it is ill manners to mention it amongst them. Be it so. But give me leave to add, that there is no ranker species of ill-breeding, than speaking of it sarcastically, or with contempt.

'Religion, strictly speaking, means the worship which men, from a sense of duty, pay to that Being unto whom they owe their own existence, with all those blessings and benefits which attend it.'

Let a man but reflect on this definition, and it will be impossible for him not to perceive the treating this in a ludicrous way, must not only be unpolite, but shocking. Who that has a regard for a man would not start at the thought of saying a base thing of his father before him? And yet what a distance is there between the notion of a father and a Creator! Since, therefore, no further arguments are necessary to prove the inconsistence between raillery and religion, what can be more cogent to a polite man, than thus showing that such discourses of his would be *mal apropos?*

Thus much for those that might be guilty of unpoliteness with respect to religion in general, a fault unaccountably common in an age which pretends to be so polite.

As to particular religions, or rather tenets in religion, men are generally warm in them, from one of these two reasons, viz. tenderness of conscience, or a high sense of their own judgments. Men of plain hearts and honest dispositions, look on salvation as too serious a thing to be jested with; a polite man, therefore, will be cautious of offending upon that head, because he knows he will give the person to whom he speaks pain; a thing very opposite to the character of a polished philosopher. The latter reason which I have assigned for men's zeal in religious matters, may seem to have less weight than the first; but he who considers it attentively will be of another opinion. Men of speculative religion, who are so from a conviction rather of their heads than their hearts, are not a bit less vehement than the real devotees. He who says a slight or a severe thing of their faith, seems to them to have thereby undervalued their understandings, and will consequently incur their aversion; which no man of common sense would hazard for a lively expression, much less a person of good-breeding, who should make it his chief aim to be well with all. As a mark of my own politeness, I will here take leave of this subject; since, by dropping it, I shall oblige the gay part of my readers, as I flatter myself I have already done the graver part, from my manner of treating it.

> Like some grave matron of a noble line,
> With awful beauty does Religion shine
> Just sense should teach us to revere the dame,
> Nor by imprudent jests to sport her fame.
> In common life you'll own this reason right,
> That none but fools in gross abuse delight:
> Then use it here—nor think our caution vain,
> To be polite, men need not be profane.

Next to their concerns in the other world, men

are usually most taken up with the concerns of the public here. The love of our country is among those virtues to which every man thinks he should pretend, and the way in which this is generally shown, is by falling into what we call parties; where, if a share of good sense allay not that heat which is naturally contracted from such engagements, a man soon falls into all the violences of faction, and looks upon every one as his enemy who does not express himself about the public good in the same terms he does. This is a harsh picture, but it is a just one, of the far greater part of those who are warm in political disputes. A polite man will therefore speak as seldom as he can on topics, where, in a mixed company, it is almost impossible to say any thing that will please all.

To say truth, patriotism, properly so called, is perhaps as scarce in this age as in any that has gone before us. Men appear to love themselves so well, that it seems not altogether credible they should, at every turn, prefer their country's interest to their own. The thing looks noble indeed; and therefore, like a becoming habit, every body would put it on. But this is hypocrisy you will say, and therefore ought to be detected. Here the Polite Philosopher finds new inducements to caution; sore places are always tender; and people at a masquerade are in pain if you do any thing which may discover their faces.

Our philosophy is not intended to make a man that sour monitor who points out folks' faults, but to make them in love with their virtues; that is, to make himself and them easy while he is with them; and to do or say nothing which, on reflection, may make them less his friends at the next meeting.

Let us explain this a little further. The rules we
offer are intended rather to guide men in company
than when alone. What we advance tends not so
directly to amend people's hearts as to regulate their
conduct ; a matter which we have already demon-
strated to be of no small importance. Yet I beg
you will observe, that though morality be not immediately our subject, we are far, however, from
requiring any thing in our pupils contrary there-
to.

A polite man may yet be religious, and, if his
reason be convinced, attached to any interest which,
in his opinion, suits best with that of the public ;
provided he conform thus far to our system, that on
no occasion he troubles others with the articles of
his religious creed or political engagements; or, by
any stroke of wit or raillery hazard for a laugh that
disposition of mind which is absolutely necessary
to make men easy when together.

Were I, indeed, to indulge my own sentiments,
I should speak yet with greater freedom on this subject. Since there is so vast a disproportion when
we come to compare those who have really either a
concern in the governments or the service of their
country more particularly at heart, and the men
who pretend to either merely from a desire of appearing of some consequence themselves, we ought
certainly to avoid making one of that number, and
aim rather at being quiet within ourselves, and
agreeable to those among whom we live, let their
political notions be what they will ; inasmuch as
this is a direct road to happiness, which all men pro-
fess they would reach if they could.—Pomponius
Atticus, whose character appears so amiable from
the concurring testimony of all who mention him,

owed the greatest part of that esteem in which he
lived, and of the reputation by which he still sur-
vives, unto his steady adherence to this rule   His
benevolence made him love mankind in general,
and his good sense hindered him from being taint-
ed with those party prejudices which had bewitched
his friends. He took not up arms for Cæsar, nor
did he abandon Italy when Pompey withdrew his
forces, and had in outward form the sanction of the
commonwealth. He saw too plainly the ambition
of both; but he preserved his complacence for his
friends in each party, without siding with either.
Success never made them more welcome to Pomponius, nor could any defeat lessen them in his esteem. When victorious he visited them, without
sharing in their power; and when vanquished he
received them, without considering any thing but
their distress. In a few words, he entertained no
hopes from the good fortune of his friends, nor suffered the reverse of it to chill his breast with fear.
His equanimity produced a just effect, and his universal kindness made him universally beloved.

I fancy this picture of a disposition perfectly free
from political sourness, will have an agreeable effect
on many of my readers, and prevent their falling
into a common mistake, that the circumstances of
public persons are the properest of topics for a general conversation; whereas they never consider
that it is hard to find a company wherein somebody
hath not either liking or distaste, or has received injuries or obligations from those who are likeliest to
be mentioned on such an occasion; and who consequently will be apt to put a serious construction
on a slight expression, and remember afterwards in
earnest, what the speaker meant so much a jest as

never to have thought of it more. These, perhaps, may pass with some trivial remarks: but with those who regard their own ease, and have at all observed what conduces to make men disagreeable to one another, I flatter myself they will have more weight.

Behaviour is like architecture; the symmetry of the whole pleases us so much, that we examine not into parts which, if we did, we should find much nicety required in forming such a structure: though, to persons of no taste, the rules of either art would seem to have little connexion with their effects.

> That true politeness we can only call,
> Which looks like Jones's fabric at Whitehall;
> Where just proportion we with pleasure see;
> Though built by rule, yet from all stiffness free;
> Though grand, yet plain; magnificent, but five;
> The ornaments adorning the design.
> It fills our mind with rational delight,
> And pleases on reflection as a slight.

After these admonitions as to religion and politics, it is very fit we observe another topic of modern discourse, of which it is hard to say whether it may be more common or more contrary to true politeness. What I mean, is the reflecting on men's professions, and play on those general aspersions which have been fixed on them by a sort of ill-nature hereditary to the world. And with this, as the third point which I promised to consider, shall be shut up the more serious part of this essay.

In order to have a proper idea of this point, we must first of all consider that the chief cause both of love and hatred is custom. When men from a

long habit, have acquired a faculty of thinking
clearly, and speaking well in any science, they naturally like that better than any other; and this liking in a short time grows up to a warmer affection, which renders them impatient whenever their
darling science is decried in their hearing. A polite man will have a care of not ridiculing physic
before one of the faculty; talking disrespectfully of
lawyers when gentlemen of the long robe are by;
or speaking contemptibly of the clergy when with
any of that order.

Some critics may possibly object that these are
solecisms of too gross a nature for men of tolerable
sense or education to be guilty of: but I appeal to
those who are more conversant in the world, whether this fault, glaring as it is, be not committed
every day.

The strictest intimacy can never warrant free-
doms of this sort; and it is indeed preposterous to
think it should, unless we can suppose that injuries
are less evils when done to us by friends, than when
they come from other hands.

Excess of wit may oftentimes beguile;
Jests are not always pardon'd by a smile;
Men may disguise their malice at the heart,
And seem at ease, the' pain'd with inward smart:
Mistaken, we think all such wounds of course
Reflection cures—alas! it makes them worse.
Like scratches, they with double anguish seize,
Rankle in time, and fester by degrees.

Let us now proceed to speak of raillery in general. Invective is a weapon worn as commonly as
a sword; and, like that, is often in the hands of
those who know not how to use it. Men of true
courage fight but seldom, and never draw but in

their own defence.   Bullies are continually squabbling; and, from the ferocity of their behaviour, become the terror of some companies, and the jest of more.   This is just the case of such as have a liveliness of thought, directed by propensity to ill-nature; indulging themselves at the expense of others, they, by degrees, incur the dislike of all. Meek tempers abhor, men of cool dispositions despise, and those addicted to choler chastise them. Thus the licentiousness of tongue, like a spirit of rapine, sets one man against all; and the defence of reputation, as well as property, puts the human species on regarding a malevolent babbler with a worse eye than a common thief; because fame is a kind of goods which, when once taken away, can hardly be restored.   Such is the effigies of this human serpent.   And who, when he has considered it, would be thought to have sat for the piece?

It is a thousand to one my book fecls the resentment of Draco, from seeing his own likeness in this glass.

A good family, but no fortune, threw Draco into the army when he was very young.   Dancing, fencing, and a smattering of the French, are all the education either his friends bestowed, or his capacity would allow him to receive.   He has been now two years in town; and from swearing, drinking, and debauching country wenches, (the general route of a military rake,) the air of St. James's has given his vices a new turn.   By dint of an embroidered coat, he thrusts himself into the beau coffee-houses, where a dauntless effrontery, and a natural volubility of tongue, conspire to make him pass for a fellow of wit and spirit.

A bastard ambition makes him envy every great

character ; and as he has just sense enough to
know that his qualifications will never recommend
him to the esteem of men of sense, or the favour of
women of virtue, he has thence contracted an an-
tipathy to both; and by giving a boundless loose to
universal malice, makes continual war against honour and reputation, wherever he finds them.

Hecatilla is a female fire-brand, more dangerous,
and more artfully vindictive, than Draco himself.
Birth, wit, and fortune, combine to render her conspicuous ; while a splenetic envy sours her otherwise amiable qualities, and makes her dreaded as a
poison doubly dangerous, grateful to the taste, yet
mortal in the effect. All who see Hecatilla at a
visit, where the brilliancy of her wit heightens the
lustre of her charms, are imperceptibly deluded into
a concurrence with her in opinion ; and suspect not
dissimulation under the air of frankness, nor a studied design of doing mischief under a seemingly casual stroke of wit. The most sacred character, the
most exalted station, the fairest reputation, defend
not from the infectious blast of sprightly raillery :
borne on the wings of wit, and supported by a blaze
of beauty, the fiery vapour withers the sweetest
blossoms, and communicates to all who hear her an
involuntary dislike to those at whose merit she
points her satire.

At ev'ning thus the unsuspecting swain,
Returning homeward o'er a marshy plain,
Pleas'd, at a distance sees the lambent light,
And, hasty, follows the mischievous sprite,
Through brakes and puddles, over hedge and style,
Rambles, misguided, many a weary mile.
Confus'd, and wond'ring at the space he's gone,
Doubts, then believes, and hurries faster on :

The cheat detected, when the vapour's spent,
Scarce he's convinced, and hardly can repent.

Next to these cautions with respect to raillery,
which, if we examine strictly, we shall find no better than a well-bred phrase for speaking ill of folks,
it may not be amiss to warn our readers of a certain
vehemence exceedingly shocking to others, at the
same time that it not a little exhausts themselves.

If we trace this error to its source, we shall find
that the spring of it is an impatience at finding
others differ from us in opinion. And can there be
any thing more unreasonable than to blame that
disposition in them which we cherish in ourselves.
If submission be a thing so disagreeable to us,
why should we expect it from them? Truth can
only justify tenaciousness in opinion. Let us calmly lay down what convinces us; and, if it is reasonable, it will hardly fail persuading those to whom
we speak. Heat begets heat; and the clashing of
opinions seldom fails to strike out the fire of dissen-
tion.

As this is a foible more especially indecent in the
fair sex, I think it will be highly necessary to offer
another, and perhaps a more cogent argument, to
their consideration. Passion is a prodigious enemy
to beauty; it ruffles the sweetest features, discolours
the finest complexion, and, in a word, gives the air
of a fury to the face of an angel. Far be it from
me to lay restraints upon the ladies; but in dissua-
ding them from this method of enforcing their sentiments, I put them upon an easier way of effecting
what they desire; for what can be denied to beauty, when speaking with an air of satisfaction? Com-
standing I consider conversation in this light, I

placence does all that vehemence would extort; as
anger can alone abate the influence of her charms.

> Serene and mild we view the evening air,
> The pleading picture of the smiling fair;
> A thousand charms our several senses meet,
> Cooling the breeze with fragrant odours sweet.
> But sudden, if the sable clouds deform
> The azure sky, and threat the coming storm,
> Hasty we flee—ere yet the thunders roar,
> And dread what we so much admired before.

To vehemence in discourse, let me join redun-
dancy in it also ; a fault flowing rather from carelessness than design, and which is more dangerous
from its being more neglected. Passion, as I have
hinted, excites opposition; and that very opposition, to a man of tolerable sense, will be the strongest reproof for his inadvertency; whereas a person
of loquacious disposition may often escape open
censure from the respect due to his quality ; or from
an apprehension in those with whom he converses,
that a check would but increase the evil, and, like
curbing a hard-mouthed horse, serve only to make
him run the faster ; from whence the person in
fault is often riveted in his error, by mistaking a silent contempt for profound attention.

Perhaps this short description may set many of
my readers right; which, whatever they may think
of it, I assure them is of no small importance.
Conversation is a sort of bank, in which all who
compose it have their respective shares. The man,
therefore, who attempts to engross it, trespasses
upon the right of his companions ; and, whether
they think fit to tell him so or no, will of consequence be regarded as no fair dealer. Notwith-

standing I consider conversation in this light, I think it necessary to observe, that it differs from other co-partnerships in one very material point, which is this, that it is worse taken if a man pays in more than his proportion, than if he had not contributed his full quota, provided he be not too far deficient; for the prevention of which, let us have Horace's caution continually in our eye.

> The indiscreet with blind aversion run
> Into one fault, where they another shun.

It is the peculiar privilege of the fair, that speaking or silent they never offend.   Who can be weary of hearing the softest harmony? or who, without pleasure, can behold beauty, when his attention is not diverted from her charms by listening to her words? I would have stopped here, but that my deference for the ladies obliges me to take notice, that some of their own sex, when past the noon of life, or in their wane of power from some other reason, are apt to place an inclination of obliging their hearers amongst those topics of detraction, by which they would reduce the lustre of those stars that now gild the hemisphere where they once shone.

From this cause only, I would advise the reigning toasts, by an equality of behaviour, to avoid the censure of these ill-natured tattlers.

> Such hapless fate attends the young and fair,
> Expos'd to open force and secret snare;
> Pursu'd by men warm with destructive fire
> Against their peace, while female frauds conspire
> Escap'd from those, in vain they hope for rest;
> What fame's secure from an invidious jest?
> By flight the deer, no more of dogs afraid,
> Falls by a shot from some dark covert made:

So envious tongues their foul intention hide;
Wound though unseen, and kill ere they're descry'd.

Of all the follies which men are apt to fall into,
to the disturbance of others and lessening of themselves, there is none more intolerable than continual egotism, and a perpetual inclination to self-pan-
egyric. The mention of this weakness is sufficient
to expose it; since, I think, no man was ever possessed of so warm an affection for his own person,
as deliberately to assert that it and its concerns are
proper topics to entertain company. Yet there are
many who, through want of attention, fall into this
vein, as soon as the conversation begins to acquire
life; they lay hold of every opportunity of introdu-
cing themselves, of describing themselves, and, if
people are so dull as not to take the hint, of commending themselves; nay, what is more surprising
than all this, they are amazed at the coldness of
their auditor, forgetting that the same passion inspires almost every body; and that there is scarce
a man in the room who has not a better opinion of
himself than of any body else.

Disquisitions of this sort into human nature belong properly unto sages in Polite Philosophy; for
the first principle of true politeness is not to offend
against such dispositions of the mind as are almost
inseparable from our species. To find out and me-
thodize these requires no small labour and application. The fruits of my researches on this subject,
I communicate freely to the public; but must, at
the same time, exhort my readers to spare now and
then a few minutes to such reflections; which will
at least be attended with this good consequence,

that it will open a scene which hath novelty (that
powerful charm) to recommend it.

But I must beware of growing serious again—I
am afraid my gravity may have disobliged some of
the *beau monde* already.

> He who intends t'advise the young and gay,
> Must quit the common road—the formal way
> Which hum-drum pedants take to make folks wise
> By praising virtue and despising vice.
> Let persons tell what dreadful ills will fall
> On such as listen when their passions call:
> We, from such things our pupils to affright,
> Say not they're sins, but that they're unpolite.
> To show their courage, beaux would often dare,
> By blackest crimes, to brave old Lucifer:
> But who, of breeding nice, of carriage civil,
> Would trespass on good manners for the devil?
> Or, merely to display his want of fear,
> Be damn'd hereafter to be laugh'd at here?

It cannot be expected from me that I should particularly criticise on all the foibles through which
men are offensive to others in their behaviour; perhaps, too, a detail of this kind, however exact,
might be thought tedious; it may be construed into
a breach of those rules, for a strict observance of
which I contend. In order, therefore, to diversify
a subject which can be no other way treated agreeably, permit me to throw together a set of characters I once had the opportunity of seeing, who will
afford a just picture of these Marplots in conversation, and which my readers, if they please, may
call the Assembly of Impertinents.

There was once a coffee-house in that end of the
town where I lodged some time ago, at which several gentlemen used to meet of an evening, who from

a happy correspondence in their humours and capacities, entertained one another agreeably from the
close of the afternoon till it was time to go to bed.

About six months this society subsisted with great
regularity, though without any restraint. Every
gentleman who had frequented the house, and con-
versed with the rectors of this occasional club, were
invited to pass an evening, when they thought fit, in
a room one pair of stairs, set apart for that purpose.

The report of this meeting drew, one night when
I had the honour of being there, three gentlemen of
distinction, who were so well known to most of the
members, that admittance could not be refused
them. One of them, whom I choose to call Major
Ramble, turned of three-score, and who had an excellent education, seized the discourse about an
hour before supper, and gave us a very copious account of the remarks he had made in three years'
travels through Italy. He began with a geographi-
cal description of the dominions of his Sardinian
Majesty as Duke of Savoy ; and, after a digression
on the fortifications of Turin, in speaking of which
he showed himself a perfect engineer, he proceeded
to the secret history of the match with Portugal, to
the abdication of King Victor Amadeus. After
this he ran over the general history of Milan, Par-
ma, and Modena ; dwelt half an hour on the adventures of the late Duke of Mantua ; gave us a
hasty sketch of the court of Rome ; transferred himself from thence to the kingdom of Naples ; repeated the insurrection of Massaniello ; and at a quarter before ten, finished his observations with the re-
cital of what happened at the reduction of that
kingdom to the obedience of the present Emperors.
What contributed to make this conduct of his the

more out of the way was, that every gentleman in the room had been in Italy as well as he; and one of them, who was a merchant, was the very person at whose house the Major resided when at Naples. Possibly he might imagine, the knowledge he had in those things might give them a great relish for his animadversions; or, to speak more candidly, the desire of displaying his own parts buried every other circumstance in oblivion.—Just as the Major had done speaking, a gentleman called for a glass of water, and happened to say, after drinking it, that he found his constitution much amended, since he left off malt-liquour. Doctor Hectic, another of the strangers, immediately laid hold of this opportunity, and gave us a large account of the virtue of water; confirming whatever he advanced from the works of the most eminent physicians. From the main subject, he made an easy transition to medicinal baths and springs. Nor were his researches bounded by our own country; he condescended to acquaint us with the properties of the springs of Bourbon; particularized the genuine smell of Spa water; applauded the wonderful effects of Piermont mineral: and, like a true patriot, wound up his disquisitions with preferring Astrop wells (within three miles of which he was born) to them all. It was now turned of eleven; when the Major and Doctor took their leaves, and went away together in a hackney-coach.

The company seemed inclinable to extend their usual time of sitting, in order to divert themselves after their night's fatigue. When Mr. Paphilio, the third new comer, after two or three severe reflections on the oddity of some people's humours, who were for imposing their own idle conceits as things

worthy the attention of a whole company; though
at the same time, their subjects are trivial, and their
manner of treating them insipid; ' for my part,'
continued he, ' gentlemen, most people do me the
honour to say, that few people understand medals
better than I do. To put the musty stories of these
queer old men out of our heads, I'll give you the history of a valuable medallion, which was sent me
about three weeks ago from Venice.' Without stay-
ing for any further remark of approbation than silence, he entered immediately on a long dissertation; in which he had scarcely proceeded ten minutes before his auditors, losing all patience, followed the example of an old Turkey merchant, who,
taking up his hat and gloves, went directly down
stairs, without saying a word

Animadversions on what I have related, would
but trespass on the patience of my reader; wherefore, in place of them, let me offer a few remarks
in verse; where my genius may be more at liberty,
and vivacity alone for want of method.

Who would not choose to shun the gen'ral scorn
And fly contempt——a thing so hardly borne?
This to avoid——let not your tales be long,
The endless speaker's ever in the wrong
All, all abhor intemperance of tongue.
Though with a fluency of easy sound,
Your copious speech with every grace abound;
Though wit adorn, and judgment give it weight,
Discretion must your vanity abate,
Ere your tir'd hearers put impatience on,
And wonder when the larum will be done.
Nor think by art attention can be wrought;
A flux of words will ever be a fault,
Things without limit we by nature blame;
And soon are cloy'd with pleasure of the same.

K

Hitherto we have dwelt only on the blemishes of conversation, in order to prevent our readers committing such offences as absolutely to destroy all pretences to politeness. But a man cannot be said to discharge the duty he owes to society who contents himself with barely doing nothing amiss: so lectures on polite philosophy, after removing these obstacles, may reasonably be expected to find out the reason whereby true politeness may be obtained. But, alas! that is not to be done by words: rocks and tempests are easily painted; but the rays of Phœbus defy the pencil.

Methinks I see my auditors in surprise. What! say they—have we attended so long in vain? have we attended to no purpose? Must we content ourselves with knowing how necessary a thing politeness is, without being able to acquire it?—Why, really, gentlemen, it is just so. I have done all for you that is in my power; I have shown you what you are not to be; in a word, I have explained politeness negatively. If you would know it positively, you must seek it from company and observation. However, to show my own good-breeding, I will be your humble servant as far as I can; that is, I will open the door for you, and introduce you, leaving you then at the single point where I can be of no further use, *id est*, application.

The world is a great school, where men are first to learn, and then to practise. As fundamentals in all sciences ought to be well understood, so a man cannot be too attentive at his first becoming acquainted with the public: for experience is a necessary qualification in every distinguished character, and is as much required in a fine gentleman as in a statesman.—Yet it is to be remarked, that experience is much sooner acquired by some than others; for it does not consist so much in a copious remembrance of whatever has happened, as in a regular attention of what may be useful; as a man is properly styled learned from his making a just use of reading, and not from his having perused a multitude of books

As soon as we have gained knowledge, we shall find the best way to improve it will be exercise; in which, two things are to be carefully avoided, positiveness and affectation. If, to our care in shunning them, we add a desire of obliging those with whom we converse, there is little danger but that we become all we wish; and politeness, by an imperceptible gradation, will enter into our minutest actions, and give a polish to every thing we do.

Near to the far-extended coasts of Spain,
Some islands triumph o'er the raging main,
Where dwelt of old—— as tuneful poets say——
Slingers, who bore from all the prize away.
While infants yet——their feeble nerves they
Nor needful food, till won by art, supplied :
Fix'd was the mark——the youngster, oft in vain,
Whirl'd the misguided stone with fruitless pain ;
Till, by long practice, to perfection brought,
With easy slight their former task they wrought.
Swift from their arm th' unerring pebble flew,
And, high in air, the fluttering victim slew.
So in each art men rise by just degrees,
And months of labour lead to years of ease

The Duke de Rochefoucalt, who was esteemed the most brilliant wit in France, speaking of politeness, says, That a citizen will hardly acquire it at court, and yet may easily attain it in the camp. I shall not enter into the reason of this; but offer

my readers a shorter, pleasanter, and more effectual method of arriving at the summit of genteel behaviour, that is, by conversing with the ladies.

Those who aim at panegyric, are wont to assem-
ble a throng of glittering ideas, and then, with great
exactness, clothe them with all the elegance of language, in order to their making the most magnifi-
cent figure when they come abroad in the world.
So copious a subject as the praises of the fair, may
in the opinion of my readers, lay me under great
difficulties in this respect.   Every man of good understanding and fine sense, is in pain for one who
has undertaken so hard a task.—Hard indeed to
me, who, from many years study of the sex, have
discovered so many perfections in them, as scarce
as many more years would afford me time to express.   However, not to disappoint my readers, or
myself, by foregoing that pleasure I feel in doing
justice to the most amiable part of the creation, I
will indulge the natural propensity I have to their
service; and paint, though it be but in miniature,
the excellencies they possess, and the accomplishments which by reflection they bestow.

> As when some poet, happy in the choice
> Of an important subject, tunes his voice
> To sweeter sounds and more exalted strains,
> Which from a strong reflection he attains—
> As Homer, while his heroes he records,
> Transfuses all their fire into his words;
> So we, intent, the charming sex to please,
> Act with new life and an unwonted ease;
> Beyond the limits of our genius soar,
> And feel an ardour quite unknown before.

Those who, from wrong ideas of things, have
forced themselves into a dislike of the sex, would

be apt to cry out, Where would this fellow run? Has he so long studied women, and does he not know what numbers of affected prudes, gay coquettes, and giddy impertinents, there are amongst them!—Alas! gentlemen, what mistakes are these? How will you be surprised, if I prove to you that you are in the same sentiments with me; and that you could not have so warm resentments at these peccadilloes if you did not think the ladies more than mortal?

Are the faults you would pass by in a friend, and smile at in an enemy, crimes of so deep a dye in them as not to be forgiven? And can this flow from any other principle than a persuasion that they are more perfect in their nature than we, and their guilt the greater, therefore, in departing even in the smallest degree, from that perfection? Or can there be a greater honour to the sex than this dignity, which even their enemies allow them, to say, truth, virtue, and women, owe less to their friends than to their foes! Since the vicious, in both cases, charge their own want of taste on the weaknesses of human nature; pursue grosser pleasures, because they are at hand, and neglect the more refined, as things of which their capacities afford them no ideas.

Born with a servile gust to sensual joy,
Souls of low taste the sacred flame destroy
By which, allied to the ethereal fire,
Celestial views the hero's thoughts inspire;
Teach him in a sublimer path to move,
And urge him on to glory and to love:
Passions which only give a right to fame,
To present bliss, and to a deathless name.
While those mean wretches, with just shame o'erspread,
Live on unknown—and are, unheard of, dead.

Mr. Dryden, who knew human nature perhaps as well as any man that ever studied it, has given us a just picture of the force of female charms in the story of Cymon and Iphigenia. Boccace, from whom he took it, had adorned it with all the tinsel of finery an Italian composition is capable of. The English poet, like most English travellers, gave sterling silver in exchange for that superficial gilding; and bestowed a moral where he found a tale. He paints, in Cymon, a soul buried in a confusion of ideas, inflamed with so little fire, as scarce to struggle under the load, or afford any glimmerings of sense. In this condition, he represents him struck with the rays of Iphigenia's beauty. Kindled by them, his mind exerts its power, his intellectual faculties seem to awake; and that uncouth ferocity of manners by which he had hitherto been distinguished, gave way to an obliging behaviour, the natural effect of love.

The moral of this fable is a truth which can never be inculcated too much. It is to the fair sex we owe the most shining qualities of which ours is master; as the ancients insinuated, with their usual address, by painting both the virtues and graces as females. Men of true taste feel a natural complaisance for women whom they converse with, and fall, without knowing it, upon every art of pleasing; which is the disposition at once the most graceful to others, and the most satisfactory to ourselves. An intimate acquaintance with the other sex, fixes this complaisance into a habit; and that habit is the very essence of politeness.

Nay, I presume to say politeness can be no other way attained. Books may furnish us with the right ideas; experience may improve our judgments;

but it is the acquaintance of the ladies only which
can bestow that easiness of address, whereby the
fine gentleman is distinguished from the scholar and
the man of business.

That my readers may be perfectly satisfied in a
point which I think of so great importance, let us
examine this a little more strictly.

There is a certain constitutional pride in men,
which hinders them from yielding in point of knowledge, honour, virtue, to one another. This immediately forsakes us at the sight of a woman. And
the being accustomed to submit to the ladies, gives
a new turn to our ideas, and opens a path to reason, which she had not trod before. Things appear in another light; and that degree of complaisance seems now a virtue, which heretofore we regarded as a meanness.

I have dwelt the longer on the charms of the sex,
arising from the perfection visible in their exterior
composition; because there is the strongest analogy
between them, and the excellencies which, from a
nicer inquiry, we discover in the minds of the fair.
As they are distinguished from the robust make of
man, by that delicacy expressed by nature in their
form; so the severity of masculine sense is softened
by a sweetness peculiar to the female soul. A
native capacity of pleasing attends them through
every circumstance of life; and what we improperly call the weakness of the sex, gives them a superiority unattainable by force.

The fable of the north wind and the sun contending to make the man throw off his cloak, is not an
improper picture of the specific difference between
the powers of either sex. The blustering fierce-

ness of the former, instead of producing the effect
at which it aimed, made the fellow but wrap up the
closer ; yet no sooner did the sun-beams play, than
that which before protected, became now an in-
cumbrance.

Just so, that pride which makes us tenacious in
disputes between man and man, when applied to
the ladies, inspires us with an eagerness not to contend, but to obey.

To speak sincerely and philosophically, women
seem designed by Providence to spread the same
splendour and cheerfulness through the intellectual
economy, that the celestial bodies diffuse over the
material part of the creation. Without them, we
might indeed contend, destroy, and triumph over
one another. Fraud and force would divide the
world between them ; and we should pass our lives
like slaves, in continual toil, without the prospect
of pleasure or relaxation.

It is the conversation of women that gives a proper bias to our inclinations, and by abating the ferocity of our passions, engages us to that gentleness of deportment which we style humanity. The
tenderness we have for them softens the ruggedness
of our own nature ; and the virtues we put on to
make the better figure in their eyes, keep us in humour with ourselves.

I speak it without affectation or vanity, that no
man has applied more assiduously than myself to
the study of the fair sex ; and I aver it with the
greatest simplicity of heart, that I have not only
found the most engaging and most amiable, but also the most generous and most heroic qualities
amongst the ladies ; and that I have discovered

more of candour, disinterestedness, and fervour, in
their friendship, than in those of our own sex,
though I have been very careful and particularly
happy in the choice of acquaintance.

My readers will, I dare say, observe, and indeed
I desire they should, a more than ordinary zeal for
inculcating a high esteem of, and a sincere attachment to, the fair. What I propose from it is, to
rectify certain notions, which are not only destructive of all politeness, but at the same time detrimental to society, and incompatible with the dignity of human nature. These have, of late years,
spread much among those who assume to themselves the title of fine gentlemen; and in consequence thereof, talk with great freedom of those
from whom they are in no danger of being called
to an account. There is so much of baseness, cowardice, and contempt of truth, in this way of treating those who are alone capable of making us truly
and rationally happy, that to consider the crime,
must be sufficient to make a reasonable man abhor
it. Levity is the best excuse for a transient slip of
this kind; but to persist in it, is evidently descend-
ing from our own species, and, as far as we are
able, putting on the brute.

Fram'd to give joy, the lovely sex are seen;
Beauteous their form, and heavenly in their mien.
Silent, they charm the pleased beholder's sight;
And speaking, strike us with a new delight:
Words, when pronounc'd by them, bear each a dart,
Invade our ears, and wound us to the heart
To no ill ends the glorious passion sways:
By love and honour bound, the youth obeys;
Till by his service won, the grateful fair
Consents, in time, to ease the lover's care;

Seals all his hopes; and in the bridal kiss,
Gives him a title to untainted bliss.

I choose to put an end to my lecture on politeness here, because having spoke of the ladies, I
would not descend again to any other subject.   In
the current of my discourse, I have taken pains to
show the use and amiableness of that art which this
treatise was written to recommend ; and have
drawn, in as strong colours as I was able, those solecisms in behaviour, which men, either through
giddiness or a wrong turn of thought, are most likely to commit.

Perhaps the grave may think I have made politeness too important a thing, from the manner in
which I have treated it : yet if they will but reflect,
that a statesman in the most august assembly, a
lawyer of the deepest talents, and a divine of the
greatest parts, must, notwithstanding, have a large
share of politeness, in order to engage the attention
and bias the inclination of his hearers, before he
can persuade them ;—they will be of another opinion, and confess, that some care is due to acquiring
that quality which must set off all the rest.

The gayer part of my readers may probably find
fault with those restraints which may result from
the rules I have here laid down.   But I would have
these gentlemen remember, that I point out a way
whereby, without the trouble of study, they may be
enabled to make no despicable figure in the world ;
which, on mature deliberation, I flatter myself they
will think no ill exchange.   The ladies will, I hope,
repay my labours, by not being displeased with
this offer of my service ; and thus having done all

in my power towards making folks agreeable to one another, I please me with the hopes of having procured a favourable reception for myself.

When gay Petronius, to correct the age?
Gave way, of old, to his satyric rage;
The motley form he for his writings chose,
And chequer'd lighter verse with graver prose.
When with just malice, he design'd to show
How far unbounded vice at last would go;
In prose we read the execrable tale,
And see the face of sin without a veil.
But when his soul, by some soft theme inspir'd,
The aid of tuneful poetry requir'd,
His numbers with peculiar sweetness ran,
And in his easy verse we see the man;
Learn'd without pride; of taste correct—yet free
Alike from niceness and from pedantry;
Careless of wealth, yet liking decent show;
In fine, by birth a wit, by trade a beau.
Freely he censur'd a licentious age.
And him I copy, though with chaster page;
Expose the evils in which brutes delight,
And show how easy 'tis to be polite;
Exhort our erring youth—to mend in time,
And lectures give, for memory's sake, in rhyme,
Teaching this art to pass through life at ease,
Pleas'd in ourselves, while all around we please.

ADVICE TO YOUTH.

SELECTED FROM THE WORKS

OF

HUGH BLAIR, D. D.

The necessity of forming religious principles at an early age.

As soon as you are capable of reflection, you must perceive that there is a right and a wrong in human actions. You see, that those who are born with the same advantages of fortune, are not all equally prosperous in the course of life. While some of them, by wise and steady conduct, attain distinction in the world, and pass their days with comfort and honour; others of the same rank, by mean and vicious behaviour, forfeit the advantages of their birth, involve themselves in much misery, and end in being a disgrace to their friends, and a burden on society. Early, then, you may learn, that it is not in the external condition in which you find yourselves placed, but on the part which you are to act, that your welfare and unhappiness, your honour or infamy, depend. Now, when beginning to act that part, what can be of greater moment, than to regulate your plan of conduct with the most serious attention, before you have yet committed any fatal or irretrievable errors? If, instead of exerting reflection for this valuable purpose, you deli-

ver yourself up, at so critical a time, to sloth and
pleasure; if you refuse to listen to any counsellor
but humour, or to attend to any pursuit except that
of amusement : if you allow yourselves to float
loose and careless on the tide of life, ready to receive any direction which the current of fashion
may chance to give you; what can you expect
to follow from such beginnings? While so many
around you are undergoing the sad consequences
of a like indiscretion, for what reason shall not these
consequences extend to you? Shall you only attain success without that preparation, and escape
dangers without that precaution, which is required
of others? Shall happiness grow up to you of its
own accord, and solicit your acceptance, when, to
the rest of mankind, it is the fruit of long cultivation,
and the acquisition of labour and care?—Deceive
not yourselves with such arrogant hopes. Whatever be your rank, Providence will not, for your
sake, reverse its established order. By listening to
wise admonitions, and tempering the vivacity of
youth with a proper mixture of serious thought, you
may ensure cheerfulness for the rest of your life;
but, by delivering yourselves up at present to giddiness and levity, you lay the foundation of lasting
heaviness of heart.

The acquisition of virtuous dispositions and habits
a necessary part of education.

When you look forward to those plans of life,
which either your circumstances have suggested, or
your friends have proposed, you will not hesitate to
acknowledge, that in order to pursue them with advantage, some previous discipline is requisite. Be

assured, that whatever is to be your profession, no
education is more necessary to your success, than
the acquirement of virtuous dispositions and habits
This is the universal preparation for every character, and every station of life. Bad as the world is,
respect is always paid to virtue. In the usual
course of human affairs it will be found, that a
plain understanding, joined with acknowledged
worth, contributes more to prosperity, than the
brightest parts without probity or honour. Whether
science, or business, or public life, be your aim, virtue still enters, for a principal share, into all those
great departments of society. It is connected with
eminence, in every liberal art; with reputation, in
every branch of fair and useful business; with distinction, in every public station. The vigour which
it gives the mind, and the weight which it adds
to character; the generous sentiments which it
breathes; the undaunted spirit which it inspires;
the ardour of diligence which it quickens; the freedom which it procures from pernicious and dishonourable avocations : are the foundations of all that
is high in fame, or great in success, among men.
Whatever ornamental or engaging endowments you
now possess, virtue is a necessary requisite, in order
to their shining with proper lustre. Feeble are the
attractions of the fairest form, if it be suspected that
nothing within corresponds to the pleasing appearance without. Short are the triumphs of wit, when
it is supposed to be the vehicle of malice. By whatever arts you may first attract the attention, you
can hold the esteem, and secure the hearts of
others, only by amiable dispositions, and the accomplishments of the mind. These are qualities
whose influence will last, when the lustre of all
that once sparkled and dazzled has passed away.

Piety to God the foundation of good morals.

Piety to God is the first thing to be recommended, as the foundation of good morals, and a disposition particularly graceful and becoming in youth. To be void of it, argues a cold heart, destitute of some of the best affections which belong to that age. Youth is the season of warm and generous emotions. The heart should then spontaneously rise into admiration of what is great; glow with the love of what is fair and excellent; and melt at the discovery of tenderness and goodness.—Where can any object be found so proper to kindle those affections, as the Father of the Universe, and the Author of all felicity? Unmoved by veneration, can you contemplate that grandeur and majesty which his, works every where display? Untouched by gratitude, can you view that profusion of good, which in this pleasing season of life, his beneficent hand pours around you. Happy in the love and affection of those with whom you are connected, look up to the Supreme Being, as the inspirer of all the friendship which has ever been shewn you by others; himself your best and your first friend; formerly, the supporter of your infancy, and the guide of your childhood; now, the guardian of your youth and the hope of your coming years. View religious homage, as a natural expression of gratitude to him for all his goodness. Consider it as the service of the God of your fathers; of him, to whom your fathers devoted you, of him whom in former ages your ancestors honoured; and by whom they are now rewarded and blessed in heaven. Connected with so many tender sensibilities of soul, let religion be with you, not the cold and barren offspring

of speculation, but the warm and vigorous dictate
of the heart.

The happiness and dignity of manhood depend up-
on the conduct of the youthful age.

Let not the season of youth be barren of improvements, which are essential to your felicity and honour. Your character is now of your own forming; your fate is, in some measure, put into your
own hands. Your nature is as yet pliant and soft.
Habits have not established their dominion. Prejudices have not pre-occupied your understanding.
The world has not had time to contract and debase
your affections. All your powers are more vigorous, disembarrassed, and free, than they will be at
any future period. Whatever impulse you now
give to your desires and passions, the direction is
likely to continue. It will form the channel in
which your life is to run; nay, it may determine
an everlasting issue. Consider, then, the employment of this important period, as the highest trust
which shall ever be committed to you; as, in a
great measure, decisive of your happiness, in time
and in eternity. As in the succession of the seasons, each, by the invariable laws of nature, affects
the production of what is next in course; so, in human life, every period of our age, according as it is
well or ill spent, influences the happiness of that
which is to follow. Virtuous youth gradually brings
forward accomplished and flourishing manhood;
and such manhood passes of itself without uneasiness, into respectable and tranquil old age. But
when nature is turned out of its regular course, disorder takes place in the moral, just as in the vege-

table world. If the spring put forth no blossoms,
in summer there will be no beauty, and in autumn
no fruit; so, if youth be trifled away without improvement, manhood will be contemptible, and old
age miserable.

On the due regulation of pleasure.

Though religion condemns such pleasures as are
immoral, it is chargeable with no improper austerity in respect of those which are innocent. By the
cautious discipline which that prescribes, think not
that it excludes you from all gay enjoyment of life.
Within the compass of that sedate spirit to which
it forms you, all that is innocently pleasing will be
found to lie. It is a mistake to imagine, that in constant effusions of giddy mirth, or in that flutter of
spirits which is excited by a round of diversions,
the chief enjoyment of our state consists. Were
this the case, the vain and frivolous would be on
better terms for happiness, than the wise, the great,
and the good. To arrange the plans of amusement, or to preside in the haunts of jollity, would
be more desirable, than to exert the highest effort of
mental powers for the benefit of nations. A consequence so absurd, is sufficient to explode the principle from which it flows. To the amusements and
lesser joys of the world, religion assigns their proper place. It admits of them, as relaxations from
care, as instruments of promoting the union of men,
and of enlivening their social intercourse. But
though it does not censure or condemn them, as
long as they are kept within due bounds; neither
does it propose them as rewards to the virtuous, or
as the principal objects of their pursuit. To such

it points out nobler ends of action. Their felicity
it engages them to seek in the discharge of an useful, and upright, and honourable part in life ; and,
as the habitual tenor of their mind, it promotes
cheerfulness, and discourages levity. Between these
two there is a wide distinction ; and the mind which
is most open to levity, is frequently a stranger to
cheerfulness. Transports of intemperate mirth are
often no more than flashes from the dark cloud ;
and in proportion to the violence of the effulgence
is the succeeding gloom. Levity may be the forced
production of folly or vice; cheerfulness is the natural offspring of wisdom and virtue only. The
one is an occasional agitation ; the other a permanent habit. The one degrades the character ; the
other is perfectly consistent with the dignity of reason, and the steady and manly spirit of religion.
To aim at a constant succession of high and vivid
sensations of pleasure, is an idea of happiness altogether chimerical. Calm and temperate enjoyment
is the utmost that is allotted to man. Beyond this,
we struggle in vain to raise our state ; and, in fact,
depress our joys by endeavouring to heighten them.
Instead of those fallacious hopes of perpetual festivity, with which the world would allure us, religion
confers upon us a cheerful tranquility. Instead of
dazzling us with meteors of joy which sparkle and
expire, it sheds around us a calm and steady light.
Let us, then, show the world, that a religious temper, is a temper sedate, but not sad ; that a religious
behaviour, is a behaviour, regulated, but not stiff
and formal. Thus we shall pass through the various changes of the world, with the least discompo-
sure ; and we shall vindicate religion from the reproaches of those who would attribute to it either

enthusiastic joys, or slavish terrors. We shall show, that it is a rational rule of life, worthy of the perfection of God, and suited to the nature and state of man.

Modesty and docility to be joined to piety.

To piety join modesty and docility, reverence of your parents, and submission to those who are your superiors in knowledge, in station, and in years. Dependence and obedience belong to youth. Modesty is one of its chief ornaments; and has ever been esteemed a presage of rising merit. When entering on the career of life, it is your part, not to assume the reins as yet into your hands; but to commit yourself to the guidance of the more experienced, and to become wise by the wisdom of those who have gone before you. Of all the follies incident to youth, there are none which either deform its present appearance, or blast the prospect of future prosperity, more than self-conceit, presumption, and obstinacy. By checking its natural progress in improvement, they fix it in long immaturity; and frequently produce mischiefs which can never be repaired. Yet these are vices too common among the young. Big with enterprise, and elated by hope, they resolve to trust for success to none but themselves. Full of their own abilities, they deride the admonitions that are given them by their friends, as the timorous suggestions of age. Too wise to learn, too impatient to be restrained, they plunge, with precipitate indiscretion, into the midst of all the dangers with which this life abounds. Positive as you now are in your opinions, and confident in your assertions, be assured, that the time approaches when both men and things will appear in a different light. Many characters which you now admire, will by and by sink in your esteem; and many opinions, of which you are at present most tenacious, will alter as you advance in years. Distrust, therefore, that glare of youthful presumption which dazzles your eyes. Abound not in your own sense. Put not yourselves forward with too much eagerness; nor imagine, that by the impetuosity of juvenile ardour, you can overturn systems which have been long established, and change the face of the world. By patient and gradual progression in improvement, you may, in due time, command lasting esteem. But by assuming at present a tone of superiority, to which you have no good title, you will disgust those whose approbation it is most important to gain. Forward vivacity may fit you to be the companion of an idle hour; but more solid qualities must recommend you to the wise, and mark you out for importance and consideration in subsequent life.

Sincerity and truth recommended.

It is necessary to recommend to you sincerity and truth. This is the basis of every virtue. That darkness of character, where we can see no heart; those foldings of art, through which no native affection is allowed to penetrate, present an object, unamiable in every season of life, but particularly odious in youth. If, at an age when the heart is warm, when the emotions are strong, and when nature is expected to show itself free and open, you can already smile and deceive; what are we to look for, when you shall be long hackneyed in the ways of men; when interest shall have completed the obduration of your heart, and when experience

shall have improved you in all the arts of guile!
Dissimulation in youth is the forerunner of perfidy
in old age. Its first appearance is the fatal omen of
future shame. It degrades parts and learning ; it
obscures the lustre of every accomplishment; and
it sinks you into contempt with God and man. As
you value, therefore, the approbation of Heaven,
or the esteem of the world, cultivate the love of
truth. In all your proceedings, be direct and consistent. Ingenuity and candour possess the most
powerful charm ; these bespeak universal favour ;
they carry an apology for almost every failing. The
path of truth is a plain and safe way ; that of falsehood, a perplexing maze. After your first depart-
ure from sincerity, it is not in your power to stop :
one artifice unavoidably leads on to another, till,
as the intricacy of the labyrinth increases, you are
left entangled in your own snare. Deceit discovers
a little mind, which stops at temporary expedi-
ents, without rising to comprehensive views of conduct. It betrays, at the same time, a dastardly
spirit. It is the resource of one who wants courage to avow his designs, or to rest upon himself.
But openness of character displays that generous
boldness which ought to distinguish youth. To set
out in the world with no other principle than a crafty attention to interest, betokens one who is destined to creep through the inferior walks of life. To
give an early preference to honour above gain,
when they stand in competition—to despise every
advantage which cannot be attained without dis-
honest arts—to brook no meanness, and to stoop to
no dissimulation—are the indications of a great
mind, the presages of future eminence and distinction in life. At the same time, this virtuous since-

rity is perfectly consistent with the most prudent
vigilance and caution. It is opposed to cunning,
not to true wisdom. It is not the simplicity of a
weak and improvident, but the candour of an en-
larged and noble mind : it is the mark of one who
scorns deceit, because he accounts it both base and
unprofitable ; of one who seeks no disguise, because
he needs none to hide him.

Benevolence and humanity.

Youth is the proper season of cultivating the be-
nevolent and humane affections. As a great part
of your happiness is to depend on the connexions
which you form with others, it is of high importance
that you acquire betimes the temper and the manners which will render such connexions comfortable. Let a sense of justice be the foundation of
all your social qualities. In your most early intercourse with the world, and even in your youthful
amusements, let no unfairness be found. Engrave
on your mind that sacred rule, of ' Doing all things
to others, according as you wish that they should
do unto you.' For this end, impress yourself with
a deep sense of the original and natural equality of
men. Whatever advantages of birth or fortune
you possess, never display them with an ostentatious superiority. Leave the subordinations of
rank, to regulate the intercourse of more advanced
years. At present it becomes you to act among
your companions, as man with man. Remember
how unknown to you are the vicissitudes of the
world ; and how often they, on whom ignorant and
contemptuous young men once looked down with
scorn, have risen to be their superiors in future

years. Compassion is an emotion of which you
ought never to be ashamed. Graceful in youth is
the tear of sympathy, and the heart that melts at
the tale of wo. Let not ease and indulgence contract your affections, and wrap you up in selfish
enjoyment. Accustom yourselves to think of the
distress of human life; of the solitary cottage, the
dying parent, and the weeping orphan. Never
sport with pain and distress in any of your amusements; never treat even the meanest insect with
wanton cruelty.

Youthful friendships.

In young minds there is commonly a strong propensity to particular intimacies and friendships.
Youth, indeed, is the season when friendships are
sometimes formed, which not only continue through
succeeding life, but which glow to the last, with a
tenderness unknown to the connexions begun in
cooler years. This propensity, therefore, is not to
be discouraged; though at the same time it must
be regulated with much circumspection and care.
Too many of the pretended friendships of youth
are mere combinations in pleasure. They are oft-
en founded on capricious likings; suddenly contracted, and as suddenly dissolved. Sometimes
they are the effect of interested compliance and flattery on the one side, and of credulous fondness on
the other. Beware of such rash and dangerous
connexions, which may afterwards load you with
shame and dishonour. Remember, that by the character of those whom you choose for your friends,
your own is likely to be formed, and will certainly
be judged of by the world. Be slow, therefore,

and cautious in contracting intimacy; but when a
virtuous friendship is once established, consider it
as a sacred engagement. Expose not yourselves to
the reproach of lightness and inconstancy, which
always bespeak either a trifling or a base mind.
Reveal none of the secrets of your friend. Be faithful to his interests. Forsake him not in danger.
Abhor the thought of acquiring any advantage by
his prejudice or hurt.

Temperance in pleasure recommended.

Let me particularly exhort youth to temperance
in pleasure. Let me admonish them to beware of
that rock on which thousands, from race to race,
continue to split. The love of pleasure, natural to
man in every period of his life, glows at this age
with excessive ardour. Novelty has fresh charms,
as yet, to every gratification. The world appears
to spread a continual feast; and health, vigour, and
high spirits, invite them to partake of it without restraint. In vain we warn them of latent dangers.
Religion is accused of insufferable severity in pro-
hibiting enjoyment; and the old, when they offer
their admonitions, are upbraided with having forgot that they once were young.—And yet, my
friends, to what do the restraints of religion, and
the counsels of age, with respect to pleasure,
amount? They may all be comprised in a few
words—not to hurt yourselves, and not to hurt
others, by your pursuit of pleasure. Within these
bounds pleasure is lawful; beyond them, it becomes
criminal: it is ruinous. Are these restraints any
other than what a wise man would choose to impose on himself? We call you not to renounce

pleasure, but to enjoy it in safety. Instead of abridging it, we exhort you to pursue it on an extensive plan. We propose measures for securing its possession, and for prolonging its duration.

On the proper management of our time.

To be impressed with a just sense of the value of time, it is highly requisite that we should introduce order into its management. Consider well, then, how much depends upon it, and how fast it flies away. The bulk of men are in nothing more capricious and inconsistent than in their appreciation of time. When they think of it as the measure of their continuance on earth, they highly prize it, and with the greatest anxiety seek to lengthen it out. But when they view it in separate parcels, they appear to hold it in contempt, and squander it with inconsiderable profusion. While they complain that life is short, they are often wishing its different periods at an end. Covetous of every other possession, of time only they are prodigal. They allow every idle man to be master of this property, and make every frivolous occupation welcome that can help them to consume it. Among those who are so careless of time, it is not to be expected that order should be observed in its distribution. But by this fatal neglect, how many materials of severe and lasting regret are they laying up in store for themselves! The time which they suffer to pass away in the midst of confusion, bitter repentance seeks afterwards in vain to recall. What was omitted to be done at its proper moment, arises to be the torment of some future season. Manhood is disgraced by the consequences of neglected youth.

L

Old age, oppressed by cares that belonged to a former period, labours under a burden not its own. At the close of life, the dying man beholds with anguish that his days are finishing, when his preparation for eternity is scarcely commenced. Such are the effects of a disorderly waste of time, in not attending to its value. Every thing in the life of such persons is misplaced.

He, on the contrary, who is orderly in the distribution of his time, takes the proper method of escaping those manifold evils. By proper management he prolongs it. He lives much in little space; more in a few years than others do in many. He can live to God and his own soul, and at the same time attend to all the lawful interests of the present world. He looks back on the past, and provides for the future. He catches the hours as they fly. They are marked down for useful purposes, and their memory remains. But by the man of confusion those hours fleet like a shadow. His days and years are either blanks, of which he has no remembrance, or they are filled up with a confused and irregular succession of unfinished transactions. He remembers indeed that he has been busy, yet he can give little account of the business which has employed him.

The necessity of depending for success on the blessing of Heaven.

Let me finish the subject, with recalling your attention to that dependance on the blessing of Heaven, which, amidst all your endeavours after improvement, you ought continually to preserve. It is too common with the young, even when they re-

solve to tread the path of virtue and honour, to set
out with presumptuous confidence in themselves.
Trusting to their own abilities for carrying them
successfully through life, they are careless of apply-
ing to God, or of deriving any assistance from what
they are apt to reckon the gloomy discipline of religion. Alas! how little do they know the dangers
which await them. Neither human wisdom, nor
human virtue, unsupported by religion, are equal
to the trying situations which often occur in life.
By the shock of temptation, how frequently have
the most virtuous intentions been overthrown?
Under the pressure of disaster, how often has the
greatest constancy sunk? Destitute of the favour
of God, you are in no better situation, with all your
boasted abilities, than orphans left to wander in
a trackless desert, without any guide to conduct
them, or any shelter to cover them from the gathering storm. Correct, then, this ill-founded arro-
gance. Expect not, that your happiness can be
independent of him who made you. By faith and
repentance, apply to the Redeemer of the world.
By piety and prayer seek the protection of the God
of Heaven.

The employment of time

Redeeming your time from those dangerous
wastes of it, which lead our youth into every disorder and confusion in society, seek to fill it with
employment which you may review with satisfaction. The acquisition of knowledge is one of the
most honourable occupations of youth! the desire
of it discovers a liberal mind, and is connected
with many accomplishments, and many virtues.

But though your train of life should not lead you to study, a course of education always furnishes proper employments to a well-disposed mind. Whatever you pursue, be emulous to excel. Generous ambition, and sensibility to praise, are, especially at your age, among the marks of virtue. Think not, that any affluence of fortune, or any elevation of rank, exempts you from the duties of application and industry. Industry is the law of our being; it is the demand of nature, of reason, and of God. Remember always, that the years which now pass over your heads, leave permanent memorials behind them. From your thoughtless minds they may escape; but they remain in the remembrance of God. They form an important part of the register of your life. They will hereafter bear testimony, either for or against you, at that day when, for all your actions, but particularly for the employment of youth, you must give an account to God. Whether your future course is destined to be long or short, after this manner it should commence; and if it continue to be thus conducted, its conclusion, at what time soever it arrives, will not be inglorious or unhappy.

Irregular pleasures.

By the unhappy excesses of irregular pleasures in youth, how many amiable dispositions are corrupted or destroyed! How many rising capacities and powers are suppressed! How many flattering hopes of parents and friends are totally extinguished. Who but must drop a tear over human nature, when he beholds that morning, which rose so bright, overcast with such untimely darkness; that good

humour, which once captivated all hearts, that vivacity which sparkled in every company, those
abilities which were fitted for adorning the highest
stations, all sacrificed at the shrine of low sensuality ; and one who was formed for running the fair
career of life in the midst of public esteem, cut off
by his vices at the beginning of his course, or sunk
for the whole of it into insignificancy and contempt?—These, O sinful Pleasure, are thy tro-
phies! It is thus that co-operating with the foe of
God and man, thou degradest human honour, and
blasteth the opening prospect of human felicity.

Industry and application.

Diligence, industry, and proper improvement of
time, are material duties of the young. To no purpose are they endowed with the best abilities, if
they want activity for exerting them. Unavailing,
in this case, will be every direction that can be giv-
en them, either for their temporal or spiritual welfare. In youth, the habits of industry are most easily acquired : in youth, the incentives to it are
strongest, from ambition and from duty, from emu-
lation and hope, from all the prospects which the
beginning of life affords. If, dead to these calls,
you already languish in slothful inaction, what will
be able to quicken the more sluggish current of ad-
vancing years? Industry is not only the instrument of improvement, but the foundation of pleasure. Nothing is so opposite to the true enjoyment
of life, as the relaxed and feeble state of an indo-
lent mind. He who is a stranger to industry, may
possess, but he cannot enjoy. For it is labour only which gives the relish to pleasure. It is the ap-
pointed vehicle of every good to man. It is the in-

dispensable condition of our possessing a sound
mind in a sound body.   Sloth is so inconsistent with
both, that it is hard to determine, whether it be a
greater foe to virtue, or to health and happiness.
Inactive as it is in itself, its effects are fatally powerful.   Though it appear a slowly-flowing stream,
yet it undermines all that is stable and flourishing,
it not only saps the foundation of every virtue, but
pours upon you a deluge of crimes and evils   It is
like water, which first purifies by stagnation, and
then sends up noxious vapours, and fills the atmos-
phere with death.   Fly, therefore, from idleness, as
the certain parent both of guilt and ruin.   And under idleness I include, not mere inaction only, but
all that circle of trifling occupations, in which too
many saunter away their youth; perpetually engaged in frivolous society, or public amusements; in
the labours of dress, or the ostentation of their persons.—Is this the foundation which you lay for future usefulness and esteem?   By such accomplishments do you hope to recommend yourselves to the
thinking part of the world, and to answer the expectations of your friends and your country?—
Amusement youth requires: it were vain, it were
cruel, to prohibit them.   But, though allowable as
the relaxation, they are most culpable as the business, of the young.   For then they become the gulf
of time, and the poison of the mind.   They foment
bad passions.   They weaken the manly powers.
They sink the native vigour of youth into contemptible effeminacy

*Unseasonable returns to the levity of youth, to be laid
aside on assuming the character of manhood.*

   To every thing, says the wise man, there is a sea-

son; and a time to every purpose under heaven.
As there are duties which belong to particular sit-
ations of fortune, so there are duties also which result from particular periods of human life. Having treated of the virtues which adorn youth, I now
call your attention to those duties which respect
manhood. I begin with observing, that the first
duty of those who are become men is ' to put away
childish things.'—The season of youthful levities,
follies, and passions, is now over.—These have had
their reign ; a reign perhaps too long ; and to which
a termination is certainly proper at last. Much indulgence is due to youth. Many things admit of
an excuse then, which afterwards become unpar-
donable. Some things may even be graceful in
youth, which, if not criminal, are at least ridiculous, in persons of maturer years. It is a great trial of wisdom to make our retreat from youth with
propriety ; to assume the character of manhood,
without exposing ourselves to reproach, by an unseasonable remainder of juvenility, on the one
hand, or by precise and disgusting formality, on the
other. Nature has placed certain boundaries, by
which she discriminates the pleasures, actions, and
employments, that are suited to the different stages
of human life. It becomes us, neither to overleap
these boundaries, by a transition too hasty and violent ; nor to hover too long on one side of the limit,
when nature calls us to pass over to the other

There are particularly two things in which middle age should preserve its distinction and separa-
tion from youth ; these are levities of behaviour,
and intemperate indulgence of pleasure. The gay
spirits of the young often prompt an inconsiderate
degree of levity, sometimes amusing, sometimes of

fensive; but for which, though betraying them occasionally into serious dangers, their want of experience may plead some excuse. A more composed
and manly behaviour is expected in riper years.
The affectation of youthful vanities degrades the
dignity of manhood; even renders its manners less
agreeable; and, by awkward attempts to please,
produces contempt. Cheerfulness is becoming in
every age. But the proper cheerfulness of a man
is as different from the levity of the boy, as the
flight of the eagle is from the fluttering of a sparrow
in the air.

As all unseasonable returns to the levity of youth
ought to be laid aside,—an admonition which
equally belongs to both sexes,—still more are we to
guard against those intemperate indulgences of
pleasure, to which the young are unhappily prone.
From these we cannot too soon retreat. They
open the path to ruin in every period of our days.
As long, however, as these excesses are confined to
the first stage of life, hope is left, that when this
fever of the spirits shall abate, sobriety may gain
the ascendant, and wiser counsels have power to
influence conduct. But after the season of youth
is past, if its intemperate spirit remains; if, instead
of listening to the calls of honour, and bending attention to the cares and the business of men, the
same course of idleness and sensuality continues to
be pursued, the case becomes more desperate. A
sad presumption arises, that long immaturity is to
prevail; and that the pleasures and passions of the
youth are to sink and overwhelm the man. Difficult, I confess, it may prove to overcome the attachments which youthful habits had for a long
while been forming. Hard, at the beginning, is the

task, to impose on our conduct restraints, which
are altogether unaccustomed and new. But this is
a trial which every one must undergo, in entering
on new scenes of action, and new periods of life.
Let those who are in this situation bethink themselves, that all is now at stake. Their character
and honour, their future fortune and success in the
world, depend in a great measure on the steps they
take, when first they appear on the stage of active
life. The world then looks to them with an observing eye. It studies their behaviour; and in-
terprets all their motions, as the presages of the line
of future conduct which they mean to hold. Now,
' therefore, put away childish things;' dismiss your
former trifling amusements, and youthful pleasures;
blast not the hopes which your friends are willing
to conceive of you. Higher occupations, more serious cares, await you.

The dangers which attend the period of middle age.

But amidst all the bustle of the world, let us not
forget to guard with vigilance against the peculiar
dangers which attend the period of middle life. It
is much to be regretted, that in the present state of
things there is no period of man's age in which his
virtue is not exposed to perils. Pleasure lays its
snares for youth: and after the season of youthful
follies is past, other temptations, no less formidable
to virtue, presently arise. The love of pleasure is
succeeded by the passion for interest. In this passion the whole mind is too often absorbed; and the
change thereby induced on the character is of no
amiable kind. Amidst the excess of youth, virtuous affections often remain. The attachments of

L 2

friendship, the love of honour, and the warmth of sensibility, give a degree of lustre to the character, and cover many a failing. But interest, when it becomes the ruling principle, both debases the mind and hardens the heart. It deadens the feeling of every thing that is sublime or refined. It contracts the affections within a narrow circle; and extinguishes all those sparks of generosity and tenderness which once glowed in the breast.

In proportion as worldly pursuits multiply, and competitions rise, ambition, jealousy and envy combine with interest to excite bad passions, and to increase the corruption of the heart. At first, perhaps, it was a man's intention to advance himself in the world by none but fair and laudable methods. He retained for some time an aversion to whatever appeared dishonourable. But here, he is encountered by the violence of an enemy. There, he is supplanted by the address of a rival. The pride of a superior insults him. The ingratitude of a friend provokes him. Animosities ruffle his temper. Suspicions poison his mind. He finds, or imagines that he finds, the artful and designing surrounding him on every hand. He views corruption and iniquity prevailing; the modest neglected, the forward and the crafty rising to distinction. Too easily, from the example of others, he learns that mystery of vice, called the way of the world. What he has learned, he fancies necessary to practise for his own defence; and of course assumes that supple and versatile character, which he observes to be frequent, and which often has appeared to him successful.

'To these, and many more dangers of the same kind, is the man exposed who is deeply engaged in

active life. No small degree of firmness in religious principle, and of constancy in virtue, is requisite, in order to prevent his being assimilated to
the spirit of the world, and carried away by 'multitude of evil doers.' Let him therefore call to
mind those principles which ought to fortify him
against such temptations to vice. Let him often
recollect that, whatever his station in life may be,
he is a man, he is a Christian. These are the chief
characters which he has to support ; characters superior far, if they be supported with dignity, to any
of the titles with which courts can decorate him ;
superior to all that can be acquired in the strife of a
busy world. Let him think, that though it may be
desirable to increase his opulence, or to advance his
rank, yet what he ought to hold much more sacred
is, to maintain his integrity and honour. If these
be forfeited, wealth or station will have few charms
left. They will not be able to protect him long
from sinking into contempt in the eye of an observing world. Even to his own eye he will at last appear base and wretched.—Let not, then, the affairs
of the world entirely engross his time and thoughts.
From that contagious air which he breathes, in the
midst of it, let him sometimes retreat into the salu-
tary shade, consecrated to devotion and to wisdom.
There, conversing seriously with his own soul, and
looking up to the Father of Spirits, let him study
to calm these unquiet passions, and to rectify those
internal disorders, which intercourse with the world
had excited and increased

On preparation for old age.

While we thus study to correct the errors, and to

provide against the dangers, which are peculiar to this stage of life, let us also lay foundation for comfort in old age. That is a period which all expect and hope to see; and to which, amidst the toils of the world, men sometimes look forward, not without satisfaction, as to the period of retreat and rest. But let them not deceive themselves. A joyless and dreary season it will prove, if they arrive at it with an unimproved or corrupted mind. For old age, as for every other thing, a certain preparation is requisite: and that preparation consists chiefly in three particulars: in the acquisition of knowledge, of friends, of virtue. There is an acquisition of another kind, of which it is altogether needless for me to give any recommendation, that of riches. But though this, by many, will be esteemed a more material acquisition than all three I have named, it may be confidently pronounced, that, without these other requisites, all the wealth we can lay up in store will prove insufficient for making our latter days pass smoothly away.

First, he who wishes to render his old age comfortable, should study betimes to enlarge and improve his mind; and by inquiry, by reading and reflecting, to acquire a taste for useful knowledge. This will provide for him a great and noble entertainment when other entertainments leave him. If he bring into the solitary retreat of age a vacant uninformed mind, where no knowledge dawns, where no ideas rise, which has nothing to feed upon within itself, many a heavy and comfortless day he must necessarily pass.—Next, when a man declines into the vale of years, he depends more on the aid of his friends, than in any other period of his life. Then is the time, when he would especially wish

to find himself surrounded by some who love and
respect him : who will bear with his infirmities, relieve him of his labours, and cheer him with their
society. Let him therefore, now, in the summer of
his days, while yet active and flourishing, by acts
of seasonable kindness and beneficence, ensure that
love, and by upright and honorable conduct lay
foundation for that respect, which in old age he
would wish to enjoy. In the last place, let him
consider a good conscience, peace with God, and
the hope of heaven, as the most effectual consolations he can possess, when the evil days shall come
wherein, otherwise he is likely to find little pleasure. It is not merely by transient acts of devotion
that such consolations are to be provided. The
regular tenor of a virtuous and pious life, spent in
the faithful discharge of all the duties of our station, will prove the best preparation for old age, for
death, and for immortality.

The conclusion

From the whole of what has been said, this important instruction arises, that the happiness of
every man depends more upon the state of his own
mind, than upon any one external circumstance ;
nay, more than all external things put together. We
have seen, that inordinate passions are the great
disturbers of life ; and that unless we possess a
good conscience, and a well-governed mind, discontent will blast every enjoyment, and the highest
prosperity will prove only disguised misery. Fix
then this conclusion in your minds, that the destruction of your virtue is the destruction of your peace.
' Keep thy heart with all diligence,' govern it with

the greatest care, ' for out of it are the issues of life.
In no station, in no period, think yourselves secure
from the dangers which spring from your passions.
Every age, and every station, they beset; from youth
to grey hairs, and from the peasant to the prince.

ON

HONOUR AS A PRINCIPLE.

BY DR. JAMES FORDYCE.

I CONCEIVE, gentlemen, that to preserve and cherish the sense of truth, integrity and glory, which we have found interwoven with the human mind, is the main design of moral culture; and that he will be the most estimable person in manhood, who is the least perverted from the ingenuity of youth; who is constantly recurring to his earliest and tenderest perceptions of virtue; who, while 'a man in understanding, is in malice a child,' who, with the improvements of reflection, and the acquisitions of experience, retains, as much as may be, that simplicity of soul, and that generosity of affection, which give such grace and sweetness to the bloom of life.

Is it possible to think of those lovely qualities, and not sigh to see them so often defaced in the succeeding scenes? Is it possible to contemplate the ruins of youthful excellence, and forbear to weep over them? But whence, my brothers, this deplorable change? From neglecting early to fix, and firmly to keep, that best and bravest of all resolutions, which was formed by one of the most celebrated persons of whom we have any record :—
'My heart shall not reproach me so long as I live.'

I will at no time, and in no situation, allow myself
in that which I suspect to be wrong. In all seasons,
and under all circumstances, I will endeavour to
practise what I feel to be right.

Many of you, I doubt not, will recollect those
memorable words of the Man of Uz; of that man
whose unblemished and unalterable worth stands
attested in a manner altogether extraordinary. The
Almighty himself we find speaking of it in a style
of exultation, if the phrase may be allowed; for
thus he is introduced addressing the enemy of all
goodness, ' Hast thou considered my servant Job,
that there is none like him in the earth, a perfect
and an upright man ?—and still he holds fast his
integrity, although thou movest me against him to
destroy him without cause.' The heaviest storm
of affliction, that ever put human virtue to the proof,
had not power to overthrow his. He might complain : it is permitted to nature. He could not
plead an entire exemption from the frailties that
will in some degree cleave to all her sons. However the benignity of his Maker might pronounce
him perfect, compared with other men, he was yc-
far enough from justifying himself in the sight of
Supreme rectitude. Those brighter discoveries
which he had obtained of the All-perfect Being,
threw him into the lowest prostrations of humility
and penitence : but nevertheless they hindered him
not from consoling himself under the weight of sor-
row, and the severity of censure, by the consciousness of a behaviour which had upon the whole been
singularly excellent and praise-worthy. Such indeed it had proved, with an uniformity that stood
the test of the most opposite conditions, and both
in the extreme.

Now what was it, think ye, next the influence of God, that could produce a conduct so superior, and so even, though thus tried? What other than the purest and noblest purpose deliberately weighed, and affectionately embraced, from the beginning? At least you will acknowledge, that characters of transcendant and persevering value are not very often formed in the advance of life, if the first part of it was passed without principle, or any vigorous sentiments of probity and honour. Is it not then most likely, that this glorious man had taken up early the magnanimous resolve before mentioned? 'My heart shall not reproach me,' that is, for any allowed transgressions or wilful neglect of its sacred dictates, 'so long as I live.'

This, my friends, and this alone, we call the principle of honour, in the truly estimable, comprehensive, and elevated sense of the expression; and we say, that the young man who sincerely adopts and steadily adheres to it, in a humble but joyful reliance on Heaven, will seldom be at a loss about the path he is to pursue, will always have at hand an answer to temptation, and will be generally fortified against those discouragements which might otherwise overwhelm him.

A youth entering the world may be compared to an unpractised traveller passing through a country, where he meets with a number of cross-roads not properly marked, which of course leave him uncertain about the right one, and, if he be not much on his guard, leads him away from it. Alas! my brothers, in how many different directions may the young, the inexperienced, and the heedless, be trained on to destruction! In just as many as there are irregular inclinations to prompt, worthless com-

panions to entice, and dangerous follies to ensnare
them. To these we may add the strange diversi-
ties of system, ' and oppositions of science, falsely
so called,' that divide and perplex mankind, in relation to the conduct which they should pursue.
Let me explain myself on this last point.

The opinions of the greater part, respecting the
track they are to follow, may be chiefly ranked in
two classes. On the one hand, you find little else
but ceremony without substance, speculation without practice, faith without works; a high flown or-
thodoxy, which, if it does not avowedly supercede
the necessity of sound morals, takes, however, all
occasions to undervalue them; and, in fine, a fiery
zeal, which burns up every sentiment of moderation and charity.'—On the other hand, you hear of
honesty without piety, good nature without real
principle, modern honour in place of old-fashioned
virtue, or, at most, certain decencies of demeanour,
that leave men at liberty to indulge the most criminal dispositions, provided only that appearances
are preserved.

If you listen to the advocates for these several
schemes, they would every one persuade you that
they, and they only, are in the right; that such as
differ from them are equally mistaken and miserable; in a word, that by espousing their party in
preference to all the rest, you can alone insure felicity. This they maintain with as much positiveness and vehemence as if truth and they were born
together. From the narrowness and partiality which
they all betray, it appears, indeed, that they are all
erroneous; yet none of them are without a multitude of followers, each system being not only pro-
pagated with a confidence that imposes, but also

adapted to smooth and screen the sinful propensities
of men, while each seems to provide some kind of
compensation : a circumstance which ought of itself to render both suspected, for this obvious reason, that complying with one obligation can never
be a just excuse for not complying with another.
But what shall we say ? Youth is a stranger to suspicion. ‘ Pausing pale Distrust,’ as the poet has
beautifully described it, ‘ the assistant of that slow
mistress Experience,’ is only to be found in the
school of the world. Fond confiding youth, yet
unacquainted with the perfidy and futility daily
practised there, is forward to believe whatever is
boldly asserted, especially if it leave a latitude,
much more if it gives encouragement to the favourite desires of nature.

But now suppose a young person hitherto uncor-
rupted, modest, simple, possessed of the amiable
dispositions which our Divine Master so much admired and applauded in children : imagine him to
hear those opposite schemes proposed and pressed
with the usual eagerness : How shall he proceed ?
What course shall he steer in this wide uncertain
ocean of contending opinions ?

There is but one safe course ; it is pointed out
by the Hand that made him, and that sent him
forth on the voyage of life : he finds it traced upon
his heart ; his reason recognises and recommends
it as the work of the Creator. ‘ He hath showed
thee, O man, what is good, and what thy Lord thy
God requireth of thee ; to do justice, to love mercy,
and to walk humbly with thy God.’ Our ingenious
inquirer listens to the voice of the Most High within him, as thus addressing his conscience : ‘ Behold, I
have placed thee in the mind of that youth, as my

representative. Fail not to exert tny power, in
blessing him with tranquility and joy, while he con
tinues his allegiance: but should he rebel, give him
to know that ' it is an evil and a bitter thing,' by
punishing him with dejection and disquietude.
Follow him every where, and make him always
sensible that his peace and welfare depends on the
veneration he entertains for God's vicegerent

Be not deceived, my young friends; he who ulti-
mately dreads any other censure than that of his
own mind, or surrenders himself implicitly to any
other direction than that of the being who made
him, may be pronounced a slave, let him pretend
to what freedom or dignity he will. He is driven
on by pride, or vanity, or interest, or inclination;
by the fear of man, or the fashion of the day, or the
caprice of the moment, or the opinion of his company, or the tone of the crowd, which he is taught
to regard as consonant to the rules of honour, if not
actually prescribing them. But consider, I beseech
you, how poor, and how precarious a conduct, to
say no worse, that must be, which is actuated by
principles so fantastic, because so variable in different men, in different nations, in different ages;
so blind in their origin, as proceeding from passion
instead of reason; and so uncertain in their effects,
as depending solely on the casual influence of education, complexion, or situation, of governments,
courts, or climates, or whatever other circumstance,
alike accidental. Is it possible, that virtue can derive solidity or steadiness from such motives; or
that any thinking man can feel security or satisfaction within, who, instead of faithfully observing
the great unerring lines of duty marked out by an
undepraved conscience, commits himself to the in-

extricable maze of human folly ? No, Gentlemen,
there is but one comprehensive, one obvious, one
immutable rule of honour, which you can follow
with safety, amidst the perilous, the changeable, the
dubious, and the partial maxims on either side, that
have been devised by self-love, worldly policy, or
false refinement. You have heard it already; but
you cannot hear it too often; it is the whole art of
acting worthily, of acting nobly, comprised in a
single short sentence; Never, while you breathe, to
offend deliberately the inward monitor—' My heart
shall not reproach me so long as I live.'

TEN PRECEPTS,

GIVEN BY

WILLIAM LORD BURGHLEY,

LORD HIGH-TREASURER OF ENGLAND,

TO HIS SON

ROBERT CECIL,

AFTERWARDS THE EARL OF SALISBURY.

———

SON ROBERT,

THE virtuous inclination of thy matchless mother, by whose tender and godly care thy infancy was governed, together with thy education under so zealous and excellent a tutor, puts me in rather assurance than hope, that you are not ignorant of that *summum bonum*, which is only able to make thee happy as well in thy death as life; I mean the true knowledge and worship of thy Creator and Redeemer, without which all other things are vain and miserable: so that, thy youth being guided by so sufficient a teacher, I make no doubt but he will furnish thy life with divine and moral documents. Yet, that I may not cast off the care beseeming a parent towards his child, or that thou shouldest have cause to derive thy whole felicity and welfare rather from others than whence thou receivedst thy breath and being, I think it fit and agreeable to the affection I bear thee, to help thee with such rules and advertisements for the squaring of thy life, as

are rather gained by experience than by much reading; to the end that, entering into this exorbitan-
age, thou mayest be the better prepared to shun
those scandalous courses whereunto the world, and
the lack of experience, may easily draw thee. And
because I will not confound thy memory, I have reduced them into ten precepts; and, next unto Mo-
ses's tables, if thou imprint them in thy mind, thou
shalt reap the benefit, and I the content. And
they are these following.

When it shall please God to bring thee to man's
estate, use great providence and circumspection in
choosing thy wife; for thence will spring all thy future good or evil : and it is an action of life, like
unto a stratagem of war, wherein a man can err
but once. If thy estate be good, match near home
and at leisure; if weak, far off and quickly. Inquire diligently of her disposition, and how her parents have been inclined in their youth. Let her
not be poor, how generous soever; for a man can
buy nothing in the market with gentility. Nor
choose a base and uncomely creature altogether for
wealth; for it will cause contempt in others, and
loathing in thee. Neither make choice of a dwarf
or a fool; for by the one thou shalt beget a race of
pigmies, the other will be thy continual disgrace;
and it will yerke thee to hear her talk: for thou
shalt find it to thy great grief, that there is nothing
more fulsome than a she-fool.

And, touching the guiding of thy house, let thy
hospitality be moderate; and, according to the
means of thy estate, rather plentiful than sparing.

but not costly; for I never knew any man grow
poor by keeping an orderly table. But some consume themselves through secret vices, and their hospitality bears the blame. But banish swinish
drunkards out of thine house, which is a vice im-
pairing health, consuming much, and makes no
show. I never heard praise ascribed to the drunkard, but for the well-bearing of his drink, which is
a better commendation for a brewer's horse or a
dray-man, than for either a gentleman or a serving
man. Beware thou spend not above three or four
parts of thy revenues, nor above a third part of that
in thy house; for the other two parts will do no
more than defray the extraordinaries, which always
surmount the ordinary by much: otherwise, thou
shalt live, like a rich beggar, in continual want.
And the needy man can never live happily nor con-
tentedly ; for every disaster makes him ready to
mortgage or sell; and that gentleman who sells an
acre of land, sells an ounce of credit : for gentility
is nothing else but ancient riches; so that if the
foundation shall at any time sink, the building must
need follow.—So much for the first precept.

II.

. Bring thy children up in learning and obedience,
yet without outward austerity. Praise them open-
ly, reprehend them secretly. Give them good countenance and convenient maintenance according to
thy ability, otherwise thy life would seem their bon-
dage; and what portion thou shalt leave them at
my death, they will thank death for it, and not
me. And I am persuaded that the foolish cocker-
ing of some parents, and the over-stern carriage of

others, causeth more men and women to take ill courses, than their own vicious inclinations. Marry thy daughters in time, lest they marry themselves. And suffer not thy sons to pass the Alps; for they shall learn nothing there but pride, blasphemy, and atheism: and if by travel they get a few broken languages, that shall profit them nothing more than to have one meat served in divers dishes. Neither, by my consent, shalt thou train them up in wars; for he that sets up his rest to live by that profession, can hardly be an honest man or a good Christian: beside, it is a science no longer in request than use; for, soldiers in peace are like chimneys in summer.

III

Live not in the country without corn and cattle about thee; for he that putteth his hand to the purse for every expense of household, is like him that keepeth water in a sieve: and what provision thou shalt want, learn to buy it at the best hand; for there is one penny saved in four, betwixt buying in thy need, and when the markets and seasons serve fittest for it. Be not served with kinsmen or friends, or men entreated to stay; for they expect much, and do little: nor with such as are amorous; for their heads are intoxicated. And keep rather too few, than one too many. Feed them well, and pay them with the most; and then thou mayest boldly require service at their hands.

IV.

Let thy kindred and allies be welcome to thy house and table. Grace them with thy coun' names, and further them in all honest actions; for by these means thou shalt so double the band of nature, as thou shalt find them so many advocates to plead an apology for thee behind thy back. But shake off those glow-worms, I mean parasites and sycophants, who will feed and fawn upon thee in the summer of prosperity; but, in the adverse storms, they will shelter thee no more than an arbour in winter.

\

Beware of suretyship for thy best friends. He that payeth another man's debts, seeketh his own decay. But if thou canst not otherwise choose, rather lend thy money thyself upon good bonds, although thou borrow it; so shalt thou secure thyself and pleasure thy friend. Neither borrow money of a neighbour or a friend, but of a stranger; where, paying for it, thou shalt hear no more of it; otherwise thou shalt eclipse thy credit, lose thy freedom, and pay as dear as to another. But in borrowing of money, be precious of thy word; for he that hath care of keeping days of payment, is lord of another man's purse.

VI.

Undertake no suit against a poor man with receiving much wrong; for, besides that thou makest him thy compeer, it is a base conquest to triumph where there is small resistance. Neither attempt law against any man before thou be fully resolved that thou hast right on thy side, and then spare not for either money or pains, for, a cause or two so followed and obtained will free thee from suits great part of thy life.

VII

Be sure to keep some great man thy friend; but trouble him not for trifles. Compliment him often with many, yet small, gifts, and of little charge. And if thou hast cause to bestow any great gratuity, let it be something which may be daily in sight; otherwise, in this ambitious age, thou shalt remain like a hop without a pole, live in obscurity, and be made a foot-ball for every insulting companion to spurn at.

VIII.

Towards thy superiors, be humble, yet generous; with thine equals, familiar, yet respective. Towards thine inferiors show much humanity, and some familiarity; as to bow the body, stretch forth the hand, and to uncover the head, with such like popular compliments. The first prepares thy way to advancement: the second makes thee known for a man well-bred: the third gains a good report, which, once got, is easily kept; for right humanity takes such deep root in the minds of the multitude, as they are easilier gained by unprofitable courtesies than by churlish benefits. Yet I advise thee not to effect or neglect popularity too much. Seek not to be Essex: shun to be Raleigh.

IX.

Trust not any man with thy life, credit, or estate; for it is mere folly for a man to enthrall himself to a friend, as though, occasion being offered, he should not dare to become thy enemy.

X.

Be not scurrilous in conversation, nor satirical in thy jests; the one will make thee unwelcome to all company, the other pulls on quarrels, and gets the hatred of thy best friends; for suspicious jests (when any of them savour of truth) leave a bitterness in the minds of those which are touched. And albeit I have already pointed at this inclusively, yet I think it necessary to leave it to thee as a special caution; because I have seen many so prone to quip and gird, as they would rather lose their friend than their jest. And, if perchance their boiling brain yield a quaint scoff, they will travail to be delivered of it as a woman with child. These nimble fancies are but the froth of wit.

THE
WAY TO WEALTH,

WRITTEN BY

DR. BENJAMIN FRANKLIN.

————

COURTEOUS READER,

I have heard that nothing gives an author so
great pleasure as to find his works respectfully quoted by others. Judge, then, how much I must have
been gratified by an incident I am going to relate
to you. I stopped my horse lately, where a great
number of people were collected at an auction of
merchants goods. The hour of sale not being
come, they were conversing on the badness of the
times; and one of the company called to a plain,
clean, old man, with white locks, "Pray, *Father
Abraham*, what think you of the times? Will not
these heavy taxes quite ruin the country? How
shall we be ever able to pay them? What would
you advise us to?"—Father Abraham stood up, and
replied, "If you would have my advice, I will give
it you in short; for, a word to the wise is enough,"
as *Poor Richard* says. They joined in desiring
him to speak his mind; and gathering round him,
he preceeded as follows :*

————

* Dr. Franklin, wishing to collect into one piece all
the sayings upon the following subjects, which he had
dropped in the course of publishing the Almanack called

'Friend,' says he, 'the taxes are indeed very heavy; if those laid on by the government were the only ones we had to pay, we might more easily discharge them: but we have many others, and much more grievous to some of us. We are taxed twice as much by our idleness, three times as much by our pride, and four times as much by our folly: and from these taxes the commissioners cannot ease or deliver us, by allowing an abatement. However, let us hearken to good advice, and something may be done for us: " God helps them that help themselves," as Poor Richard says.

1. ' It would be thought a hard government that should tax its people one-tenth part of their time to be employed in its service: but idleness taxes many of us much more: sloth, by bringing on diseases, absolutely shortens life. " Sloth, like rust, consumes faster than labour wears, while the used key is always bright," as Poor Richard says.—" But dost thou love life? then do not squander time, for that is the stuff life is made of," as Poor Richard says. How much more than is necessary do we spend in sleep; forgetting that, " The sleeping fox catches no poultry," and " there will be sleeping enough in the grave," as Poor Richard says.

" If time be of all things the most precious, wasting time must be," as Poor Richard says, " the

---

Poor Richard, introduced *Father Abraham* for this purpose. Hence it is, that Poor Richard is so often quoted. Notwithstanding the stroke of humour in the concluding paragraph of this address, Poor Richard [Saunders] and Father Abraham have proved in America, that they are no *common* preachers. And shall we, brother Englishmen, refuse good sense and saving knowledge, because it comes from the other side of the water?

greatest prodigality;" since, as he elsewhere tells
us, " Lost time is never found again ; and what we
call time enough always proves little enough."

' Let us then up and be doing, and doing to the
purpose : so by diligence we shall do more with less
perplexity. " Sloth makes all things difficult, but
industry all easy ; and he that riseth late, must trot
all day, and shall scarce overtake his business at
night ; while laziness travels so slowly, that poverty soon overtakes him. Drive thy business, let not
that drive thee ; and early to bed, and early to rise,
makes a man healthy, wealthy, and wise," as Poor
Richard says.

' So what signifies wishing and hoping for better
times ; we may make these times better, if we bo-
stir ourselves. " Industry need not wish ; and he
that lives upon hope will die fasting. There are no
gains without pains ; then help, hands, for I have
no lands ;" or, if I have, they are smartly taxed.
" He that hath a trade, hath an estate ; and he that
hath a calling, hath an office of profit and honour,"
as Poor Richard says ; but then the trade must be
worked at, and the calling well followed, or neither
the estate nor the office will enable us to pay our
taxes. If we are industrious we shall never starve ;
for, " At the working man's house hunger looks in,
but dares not enter." Nor will the bailiff or the
constable enter ; for, " Industry pays debts, while
despair increaseth them." What though you have
found no treasure, nor has any rich relation left
you a legacy, " Diligence is the mother of good
luck, and God gives all things to industry. Then
plough deep, while sluggards sleep, and you shall
have corn to sell and to keep." Work while it is
called to-day, for you know not how much you

may be hindered to-morrow. "One to-day is worth two to-morrows,' as Poor Richard says; and farther, "Never leave that till to-morrow, which you can do to-day."—If you were a servant, would you not be ashamed that a good master should catch you idle? Are you then your own master? Be ashamed to catch yourself idle, when there is so much to be done for yourself, your family, your country, and your king. Handle your tools without mittens; remember, that, "The cat in gloves catches no mice," as Poor Richard says. It is true there is much to be done, and, perhaps, you are weak-handed; but stick to it steady, and you will see great effects; for "Constant dropping wears away stones; and, by diligence and patience, the mouse ate in two the cable; and little strokes fell great oaks."

'Methinks I hear some of you say, "Must a man afford himself no leisure?" I will tell thee, my friend, what Poor Richard says: "Employ thy time well, if thou meanest to gain leisure; and, since thou art not sure of a minute, throw not away an hour." Leisure is time for doing something useful; this leisure the diligent man will obtain, but the lazy never; for, "A life of leisure and a life of laziness are two things." Many without labour would live by their wits only, but they break for want of stock; whereas industry gives comfort, and plenty, and respect. "Fly pleasures, and they will follow you. The diligent spinner has a large shift; and, now I have a sheep and a cow, every body bids me good-morrow."

II. But with our industry we must likewise be steady, settled, and careful, and oversee our own

affairs with our own eyes, and not trust too much
to others; for, as Poor Richard says.

> " I never saw an oft-removed tree,
> Nor yet an oft-removed family,
> That throve so well as those that settled be."

‘ And again, " Three removes are as bad as a
fire;" and again, " Keep thy shop, and thy shop
will keep thee ;" and again, " If you would have
your business done, go ; if not, send." And again,

> " He that by the plough would thrive,
> Himself must either hold or drive."

‘ And again, " The eye of the master will do more
work than both his hands;" and again, " Want
of care does us more damage than the want of
knowledge ;" and again, " Not to oversee work-
men, is to leave them your purse open." Trusting
too much to others' care is the ruin of many; for,
in the affairs of this world, men are not saved by
faith, but by the want of it : but a man's own care
is profitable ; for, " If you would have a faithful
servant, and one that you like, serve yourself: a
little neglect may breed great mischief: for want of
a nail the shoe was lost; for want of a shoe, the
horse was lost ; and for want of a horse, the rider
was lost," being overtaken and slain by the enemy;
all for want of a little care about a horse-shoe nail.

III. ‘ So much for industry, my friends, and attention to one's own business : but to these we must
add frugality, if we would make our industry more
certainly successful. A man may, if he knows not
how to save as he gets, " keep his nose all his life to
the grindstone, and die not worth a groat at last.
A fat kitchen makes a lean will."

M 2

> " Many estates are spent in getting,
> Since women for tea forsook spinning and knitting,
> And men for punch forsook hewing and splitting."

" If you would be wealthy, think of saving as
well as of getting. The Indies have not made Spain
rich, because her out-goes are greater than her in-
comes."

' Away, then, with your expensive follies, and
you will not then have so much reason to complain
of hard times, heavy taxes, and chargeable families; for,

> " Women and wine, game and deceit,
> Make the wealth small and the want great.'

And farther, " What maintains one vice would
bring up two children." You may think, perhaps,
that a little tea, or a little punch now and then, diet
a little more costly, clothes a little finer, and a little
entertainment now and then, can be no great mat
ter; but remember, " Many a little makes a mickle:"
beware of little expenses; " a small leak will sink a
great ship," as Poor Richard says; and again,
" Who dainties love, shall beggars prove;" and
moreover, " Fools make feasts, and wise men eat
them." Here you are all got together to this sale
of fineries and nicknacks. You call them *goods ;*
but, if you do not take care, they will prove *evils* to
some of you. You expect they will be sold cheap,
and perhaps they may for less than they cost ; but
if you have no occasion for them, they must be
dear to you. Remember what Poor Richard says,
" Buy what thou hast no need of, and ere long thou
shalt sell thy necessaries." And again, " At a great
penny-worth pause a while." He means, that perhaps the cheapness is apparent only, and not real;

or the bargain, by straitening thee in thy business, may do thee more harm than good. For in another place he says, "Many have been ruined by buying good penny-worths." Again, "It is foolish to lay out money in a purchase of repentance;" and yet this folly is practised every day at auctions, for want of minding the Almanack. Many a one, for the sake of finery on the back, has gone with a hungry belly, and half-starved their families; "Silks and satins, scarlets and velvets, put out the kitchen fire," as Poor Richard says. These are not the necessaries of life, they can scarcely be called the conveniences; and yet, only because they look pretty, how many want to have them! By these and other extravagances, the genteel are reduced to poverty, and forced to borrow of those whom they formerly despised, but who, through industry and frugality, have maintained their standing; in which case it appears plainly, that "A ploughman on his legs is higher than a gentleman on his knees," as Poor Richard says. Perhaps they have had a small estate left them, which they knew not the getting of; they think, "It is day, and will never be night;" that a little to be spent out of so much is not worth minding; but "Always taking out of the meal-tub, and never putting in, soon comes to the bottom," as Poor Richard says; and then, "When the well is dry, they know the worth of water." But this they might have known before, if they had taken his advice; "If you would know the value of money, go and try to borrow some; for he that goes a borrowing goes a sorrowing," as Poor Richard says; and, indeed, so does he that lends to such people, when he goes to get it in again. Poor Dick farther advises and says.

" Fond pride of dress is sure a very curse;'
Ere fancy you consult, consult your purse."

' And again. " Pride is as loud a beggar as want,
and a great deal more saucy." When you have
bought one fine thing, you must buy ten more, that
your appearance may be all of a piece; but Poor
Dick says, " It is easier to suppress the first desire,
than to satisfy all that follow it;" and it is as truly
folly for the poor to ape the rich, as for the frog to
swell, in order to equal the ox.

" Vessels large may venture more,
But little boats should keep near shore."

' It is, however, a folly soon punished: for, as
Poor Richard says, " Pride that dines on vanity,
sups on contempt :—Pride breakfasted with Plenty,
dined with Poverty, and supped with Infamy."
And after all, of what use is this pride of appearance, for which so much is risked, so much is suffered ? It cannot promote health, nor ease pain ·
it makes no increase of merit in the person; it cre-
ates envy, it hastens misfortune.

' But what madness must it be to *run* in *debt* for
these superfluities? We are offered, by the terms
of this sale, six months credit; and that, perhaps,
has induced some of us to attend it, because we
cannot spare the ready money, and hope now to be
fine without. But, ah! think what you do when
you run in debt; you give another power over your
liberty; if you cannot pay at the time, you will be
ashamed to see your creditor; you will be in fear
when you speak to him; you will make poor piti-
ful sneaking excuses, and by degrees come to lose
your veracity, and sink into base downright lying;
for, " The *second* vice is lying, the first is running

in debt," as Poor Richard says; and again to the
same purpose, "Lying rides upon Debt's back:"
whereas, a free-born Englishman ought not to be
ashamed or afraid to see or speak to any man living. But poverty often deprives a man of all spirit
and virtue. " It is hard for an empty bag to stand
upright." What would you think of that prince, or
of that government, who should issue an edict for-
bidding you to dress like a gentleman or gentlewo-
man on pain of imprisonment or servitude ? Would
you not say that you were free, have a right to dress
as you please, and that such an edict would be a
breach of your privileges, and such a government
tyrannical? And yet you are about to put yourself under that tyranny, when you run in debt for
such dress? Your creditor has authority, at his
pleasure, to deprive you of your liberty, by confi-
ning you in jail for life, or by selling you for a servant, if you should not be able to pay him. When
you have got your bargain, you may, perhaps, think
little of payment ; but, as Poor Richard says, " Cre-
ditors have better memories than debtors ; credi-
tors are a superstitious sect, great observers of set
days and times." The day comes round before
you are aware, and the demand is made before you
are prepared to satisfy it: or, if you bear your
debt in mind, the term, which at first seemed so
long, will, as it lessens, appear extremely short.
Time will seem to have added wings to his heels as
well as his shoulders. "Those have a short Lent,
who owe money to be paid at Easter." At present, perhaps, you may think yourselves in thri-
ving circumstances, and that you can bear a little
extravagance without injury ; but

" For age and want save while you may
   No morning sun lasts a whole day."

' Gain may be temporary and uncertain, but, ever
while you live, expense is constant and certain;
and, " It is easier to build two chimneys, than
to keep one in fuel," as Poor Richard says; so,
" Rather go to bed supperless, than rise in debt."

" Get what you can, and what you get hold,
   'Tis the stone that will turn all your lead into gold.

' And, when you have got the philosopher's stone,
sure you will no longer complain of bad times or
the difficulty of paying taxes.

IV. ' This doctrine, my friends, is reason and
wisdom. But after all, do not depend too much
upon your own industry, and frugality, and prudence, though excellent things; for they may be all
blasted, without the blessing of Heaven; and, therefore, ask that blessing humbly, and be not unchari-
table to those that at present seem to want it, but
comfort and help them. Remember Job suffered,
and was afterwards prosperous.

' And now to conclude, " Experience keeps a
dear school, but fools will learn in no other," as
Poor Richard says, and scarcely in that; for, it is
true, " We may give advice, but we cannot give
conduct :" However, remember this, " They that
will not be counselled cannot be helped !" and farther, that, " If you will not hear Reason, she will
surely rap your knuckles," as Poor Richard says.'

Thus the old gentleman ended his harangue.
The people heard it, and approved the doctrine,—
and immediately practised the contrary, just as if
it had been a common sermon; for the auction

opened, and they began to buy extravagantly.—I found the good man had thoroughly studied my Almanacks, and digested all I had dropped on these topics during the course of twenty-five years. The frequent mention he made of me must have tired any one else; but my vanity was wonderfully delighted with it, though I was conscious, that not a tenth part of the wisdom was my own, which he ascribed to me; but rather the gleanings that I had made of the sense of all ages and nations. However, I resolved to be the better for the echo of it; and, though I had at first determined to buy stuff for a new coat, I went away resolved to wear my old one a little longer. Reader, if thou wilt do the same, thy profit will be as great as mine.

I am, as ever,

Thine to serve thee,

RICHARD SAUNDERS.

THE
UNIVERSAL PRAYER.

BY A. POPE, ESQ.

FATHER of all! in ev'ry age,
  In ev'ry clime ador'd,
By saint, by savage, and by sage,
  Jehovah, Jove, or Lord.

Thou great first cause, least understood,
  Who all my sense confin'd
To know but this,—that Thou art good
  And that myself am blind.

Yet gave me, in this dark estate
  To see the good from ill;
And binding nature fast in fate,
  Left free the human will.

What conscience dictates to be done,
  Or warns me not to do,
This, teach me more than hell to shun,
  That, more than heav'n pursue.

What blessings thy free bounty gives,
  Let me not cast away;
For God is paid when man receives,
  T' enjoy is to obey.

Yet not to earth's contracted span
  Thy goodness let me bound,
Or think thee Lord alone of man,
  When thousand worlds are round.

Let not this weak unknowing hand,
    Presume thy bolts to throw,
Or deal damnation round the land,
    On each I judge thy foe.

If I am right, O teach my heart
    Still in the right to stay,
If I am wrong, thy grace impart
    To find the better way.

Save me alike from foolish pride
    Or impious discontent,
At ought thy wisdom has deny'd
    Or ought thy goodness lent.

Teach me to feel another's woe,
    To hide the faults I see!
The mercy I to others show,
    That mercy show to me.

Mean though I am, not wholly so,
    Since quicken'd by thy breath
O lead me wheresoe'r I go,
    Through this day's life or death.

This day be bread and peace my lot ;
    All else beneath the sun
Thou know'st if best bestow'd or not,
    And let thy will be done.

To Thee, whose temper is all space,
    Whose altar—earth, sea, skies ;
One chorus let all beings raise ;
    All nature's incense rise.

THE END.

CPSIA information can be obtained at www.ICGtesting.com
Printed in the USA
LVOW081312120212

268301LV00021B/192/A